Drama Classics

W9-ANW-132

The Drama Classics series aims to offer the world's greatest plays in affordable paperback editions for students, actors and theatregoers. The hallmarks of the series are accessible introductions, uncluttered and uncut texts and an overall theatrical perspective.

Given that readers may be encountering a particular play for the first time, the introduction seeks to fill in the theatrical/historical background and to outline the chief themes rather than concentrate on interpretational and textual analysis. Similarly the play-texts themselves are free of footnotes and other interpolations: instead there is an end-glossary of 'difficult' words and phrases.

The texts of the English-language plays in the series have been prepared taking full account of all existing scholarship. The foreign language plays have been newly translated into a modern English that is both actable and accurate: many of the translators regularly have their work staged professionally.

Under the editorship of Kenneth McLeish, the Drama Classics series is building into a first-class library of dramatic literature representing the best of world theatre.

Series editor: Kenneth McLeish

Associate editors:

Professor Trevor R. Griffiths, *School of Literary and Media Studies, University of North London*

Simon Trussler, *Reader in Drama, Goldsmiths' College, University of London*

DRAMA CLASSICS *the first hundred*

*The publishers welcome
suggestions for further titles*

DRAMA CLASSICS

VOLPONE

by

Ben Jonson

introduced by Colin Counsell

I am my own
wife #47

IWDMX 52

may 25

Lycium Theatre

149 W 45th

212 9478844

NICK HERN BOOKS

London

A Drama Classic

This edition of *Volpone* first published in Great Britain
as a paperback original in 1995 by Nick Hern Books Limited,
14 Larden Road, London W3 7ST

Text reproduced from the 'Revels Plays' edition of *Volpone*,
R.B Parker (ed.), Manchester University Press , 1983.
By permission.

Typeset by Country Setting, Woodchurch, Kent TN26 3TB
Printed by BPC, Hazell Books Limited, Aylesbury HP20 1LB

A CIP catalogue record for this book is available from the
British Library

ISBN 1 85459 194 0

Introduction

Ben Jonson (1572-1637)

Jonson was born in London a month after the death of his minister father. While he was still a youth, his mother remarried, this time to a master builder. Jonson was apprenticed to a bricklayer, but he disliked the trade so much that he soon left to join the English forces fighting in Flanders. During a lull in hostilities, he challenged a member of the opposing army to single combat, killing him and bearing back his arms as a sign of victory.

This chapter of adventure was to prove not untypical of Jonson's life. Returning to England, Jonson joined a company of strolling players, making his living as an actor until, in 1597, he was employed as a playwright by Philip Henslowe, manager of one of London's leading theatre companies, the Admiral's Men. A year later in 1598 the success of his comedy, *Every Man in his Humour*, established him as one of the leading dramatists of Renaissance England.

Any euphoria resulting from this success must have been short-lived. Following an argument with a member of the company, Jonson duelled with the man, killing him despite the fact that, as the playwright himself noted, his opponent's sword was ten inches longer than his own. Sent to prison, he avoided execution only by pleading 'benefit of clergy', an ancient law by which a literate man could have a death sentence commuted to the branding of his thumb and confiscation of all his goods. This was neither the first nor last time Jonson experienced imprisonment. He had already been gaoled briefly for his part in the writing of *The Isle of Dogs* (c.1597), a play condemned as seditious and slanderous, and was later to suffer the same punishment for his involvement with *Eastward Ho!* (1605), whose satire of the Scots unsurprisingly found little favour with the newly invested, Scots-born monarch, James I. Nevertheless the next sixteen years saw a string of comic successes from Jonson, including *Every*

Man Out of His Humour (1599), *Volpone* (1605-6), *Epicoene or The Silent Woman* (1609-10), *The Alchemist* (1610) and *Bartholomew Fair* (1614).

Jonson's tragedies *Sejanus* (1603) and *Catiline* (1611) were received with less enthusiasm, being considered too verbose and learned. But despite his early brush with regal displeasure, the masques he wrote for King James – spectacular court entertainments, produced in a stormy collaboration with designer Inigo Jones – were as highly praised as his comedies, and Jonson soon became a well-known figure of London society. Although his declining years were dogged by periodic illness and debt, and his late works have not proved as durable as some of his early ones, he nevertheless did more to influence the drama of the Restoration period than any other English writer. When he died in 1637 he was buried in Westminster Abbey – a signal honour – and it is reported that his body was followed to its grave by the greater part of fashionable London society.

Volpone: **What Happens in the Play**

Volpone ('Fox') is a 'magnifico', a Venetian aristocrat, who has hit on a plan to increase his already substantial wealth. By pretending to be mortally ill he whets the mercenary appetites of his fellow citizens, who hanker to become his heir. Egged on by Volpone's servant Mosca ('Fly'), Voltore ('Vulture') the advocate, Corvino ('Crow') the merchant, the old gentleman Corbaccio ('Raven') and Lady Politic Would-be visit the supposedly ailing man bearing rich gifts, for with such tokens of 'friendship' each hopes to benefit from Volpone's will when he dies. By exploiting his fellow Venetians' greed, Volpone increases his own wealth – and indeed, there seems no limit to how far the four will go to lay hands on his fortune. Corbaccio disinherits his son, Bonario, instead naming Volpone in his will. Voltore and Lady Would-be perjure themselves in court. Corvino is even cajoled into offering his wife, the beautiful and virtuous Celia, as Volpone's sexual partner as part of a spurious 'cure' for the magnifico's ills.

Delighting in his intrigues and determining to torment his ghoulish neighbours still further, Volpone spreads the news that he has died and left all his goods to Mosca. But it is here that the Fox's cunning fails him. Mosca is every bit as wily as he is, and uses the ploy in an attempt to secure his 'dead' master's fortune for himself. In a spectacular reversal of fortunes in the final scene, the pair fall out, each revealing the other's duplicity to the assembled Venetians and thus delivering themselves into the hands of justice.

Jonsonian Comedy

Jonson was the great populist playwright of the late sixteenth and early seventeenth century in England, the chronicler of the life and values of ordinary people. His comic works reflect the spirit of 'Carnival', a culture of fairs and festivals in which the normal rules of society were suspended. During Carnival hierarchies of social status were ignored, and the prevailing political and religious order was mocked and turned upside-down. Carnival instead celebrated the communal life of the people and the pleasures of the body – eating, drinking and sex.

Jonson's works are full of varied, often coarse, street slang, capturing the noise and vibrancy of life in the teeming London of his time. They show us characters from all levels of society: not only aristocrats and gentry, but tradesmen and hawkers, thieves, mountebanks and prostitutes. Similarly, his main characters rarely embody Renaissance aristocratic and Christian ideals. Most often they are likable rogues, people who thrive through guile and energy, turning upside-down the ruling values of their society and so satisfying a popular desire to see authority overturned.

Volpone himself is a case in point. He is hardly a laudable figure – a scoundrel whose greatest pleasure is to cheat others. None the less, our disapproval is always offset by the even worse behaviour of those who hope to benefit by his death: they too are cheats and liars, but far less skilled than he is. Moreover, unlike them, Volpone is motivated less by plain avarice than by the delight he takes in the game – as he tells Mosca, 'I glory more in the cunning purchase of my wealth / Than in the glad possession.' The play's first moments make it clear that, although he hoards his treasure, he does so for the sheer sensuous pleasure it brings him, and such sensuousness is the keynote of his character. He demands that his servants entertain him with songs and dances, and promises Celia such exotic pleasures as a bath of 'spirit of roses, and of violets, / The milk of unicorns, and panthers' breath', and a banquet including 'the heads of parrots, tongues of nightingales, / The brains of peacocks'. He is a 'voluptuary', one devoted to extravagant and emphatically physical pleasures, and so implicitly opposed to the abstemiousness of official Christian culture. If he is a rogue, he is a rogue in Falstaff style, displaying a vitality and a delight in life that make him the play's most attractive character.

Carnival gusto is only one side of Jonson's drama, for he was also a learned man, one of the leading neoclassicists of the English Renaissance stage. His plays regularly use ideas and images from classical myth and quote the writings of such classical authors as Aristotle and Juvenal; he is clearly also familiar with Greek 'New Comedy', as adapted by the Roman poets Plautus and Terence.

This familiarity with ancient Greek and Roman models was common in English culture of the period. Indeed, in his book *The Defense of Poesie* (1595), Sir Philip Sidney argued for, among other things, a return to the aesthetic principles established by classical authors – advice which undoubtedly had an impact upon Jonson's work. *Volpone*, for example, for the most part obeys the 'unities' of time, place and action which Aristotle was generally supposed to have prescribed: its events occur during one day, in one city, and, although not all are part of a single storyline – the play features a subplot – all are unified thematically.

More important perhaps is the very model of comedy that Jonson uses. Many comedies of the period, including those of Shakespeare, conclude with marriages, presenting the audience with a vision of unity in which heroes and villains join together, conflicts forgiven, in a reaffirmation of social harmony. But Sidney deplored what he called such 'mongrel' mixtures: according to the classical model, comedy should be a vehicle for social criticism. By ridiculing humankind's imperfections, and dramatising their punishment, it should help cleanse society of flaws. This view of comedy informs much of Jonson's writing, and provides the logic for the conclusion of *Volpone*. The play ends with all the nefarious characters subject to poetically just retribution. The dissembling Mosca is made a galley slave and Volpone is imprisoned in a 'hospital of the Incurabili', while each of those who sought to become his heir is punished in a way appropriate to their particular transgression. Only the morally untainted characters, Celia and Bonario, emerge unscathed from the play's dénouement, so offering a vision of virtue's triumph – and they fail to pair off with one another, a complete departure from the usual procedure in romantic comedy.

The influence of classical New Comedy is also evident in the very characters Jonson creates. Whereas in Shakespeare's comedies characters can be seen as psychologically detailed or 'rounded', the denizens of New Comedy were 'flat'. Plautus in particular peopled his plays largely with stock characters, each defined by a single, dominant characteristic. It is creations of this kind that we find most often in Jonson's work, including *Volpone*. Aside from Volpone himself, and perhaps Mosca, the inhabitants of Jonson's Venice are less individuals than 'types': Corbaccio is a foolish old man, somewhat similar to the 'senex' of Roman comedy, Corvino is an archetypal jealous husband, and so on.

In this respect such characters also conform to another dramatic form, one generally considered to have been created by Jonson himself, the 'Comedy of Humours'. According to the accepted medical wisdom of the Renaissance, the human body contained four distinct fluids: blood, phlegm, yellow bile and black bile. When in balance, these fluids produced a 'balanced' personality, one in which the diverse facets of human character were in proportion. But an imbalance caused exaggerated personality traits – if a person had too much black bile he or she was melancholic ('black-bilious'), an excess of phlegm resulted in a character that was 'phlegmatic', too much blood made one sanguine ('bloody') or cheerful, while a high proportion of yellow bile made for a 'choleric' bad-temper. This idea offered a way of describing human personality, and so gave dramatists a means of organising character. But although all Jonson's comic works feature characters who are driven by a different obsession or *idée fixe*, in *Volpone* almost all are driven by one single emotion: greed.

Greed and Deception

The theme of greed is evident from Volpone's, and the play's, very first words – 'Good morning to the day; and next, my gold!'.

Volpone follows these words with a 25-line speech in praise of gold, arguing that wealth far transcends 'All style of joy in children, parents, friends / Or any other waking dream on earth', and referring to gold sacrilegiously as a 'relic', a 'god' and a 'saint'; his treasure is 'sacred' and its hiding place a 'shrine'. As well as revealing something of Volpone's character, this opening effectively predicts the play's final outcome: Volpone is avaricious to the point of blasphemy, and the story can conclude satisfactorily only when he has been justly punished.

The way greed motivates Volpone's world is further emphasised by the importance of material possessions in this play. Objects and lists of objects abound. Mosca reads an inventory of Volpone's goods to torment the quartet of would-be inheritors; Volpone tries to seduce Celia by listing all manner of sumptuous, exotic delights; Sir Politic Would-be hatches scheme after scheme to win mercantile riches; even medicine leads to lists of many and arcane ingredients. It is not only Volpone who makes a god of gold; the importance of material possessions in the lives of almost all the characters indicates the mortal sin to which they have fallen prey.

Greed in *Volpone* is shown to us not only in language – theatre is a performing art in which sight is as important as sound. Having delivered the play's initial lines, Volpone immediately commands the opening of a curtain to reveal his hidden hoard of treasure. Thus the audience too is treated to a glimpse of shining gold, introduced to that sensuous pleasure which enchants the Fox. The play continues with a sequence of visits, each of Volpone's aspiring heirs bringing him some rich jewel. The jewels provide a focus not only for the characters' machinations but also for the audience's attention; in following the action, we in the auditorium are also beguiled by gold.

But if greed lies at the heart of *Volpone*, so does the deception that results from it. Deception is the basis of the entire plot: Volpone's scheme of pretending to be an invalid at death's door is only the first of several guises he adopts. In order to catch a glimpse of Celia, Volpone impersonates a famous travelling hawker of medicines (or 'mountebank'), Scoto of Mantua; he takes on the guise of an officer (or 'Commendatore') to observe the discomfort of his disappointed 'heirs' without being recognised; to wring the final drops of pleasure

from his intrigues, he even 'plays' his dead self, hiding so as to witness the scavengers' disappointment. Most other characters employ
similar deceptions – for example, Voltore, Corbaccio, Corvino and
Lady Would-be pretend to be friends of Volpone concerned for his
failing health.

Dissembling of various kinds was a common feature of Renaissance
drama. The plays of the period are filled with young women who
dress as boys to escape detection, rulers who adopt humble guises to
see the workings of their realm without being recognised, and diverse
plots involving the adoption of false identities. Shakespeare's *The
Comedy of Errors*, involving two identical-twin masters and two
identical-twin servants, is by no means untypical. But in Jonson's
play such misrepresentation is more than merely a device for
furthering comic action. In *Volpone*, disguise, deception and false
identity are the fruits of corruption, emblematic of the dishonesty to
which greed leads.

Misrepresentation is at the centre of even the play's subplot of
Peregrine and Sir Politic Would-be. Sir Politic's surname is as apt as
those of the other characters, for with his tall stories and improbable
schemes for trade he seeks to present himself as the man he would-
be, the seasoned traveller wise to the ways of Venice and well able to
advance his own fortunes in the world. But his schemes are ludicrous,
his claims transparently false, and together they effectively reveal
Sir Politic to be no more than a braggart. The punishment to which
Peregrine finally subjects him is deliberately appropriate, like the
torments visited upon Volpone and the others. Believing that he is
sought by the Venetian authorities, Sir Politic is tricked into adopting
a real disguise, that of a tortoise: a 'role' no more implausible than the
ones he has chosen for himself and every bit as easy to see through.

It is a mark of Jonson's dramatic skill that he is able to incorporate all
these deceptions and fabrications of identities and situations into his
use of the theatrical medium itself. As spectators we agree to accept
that the figure who stands before us is not an actor but a character;
we accept the theatrical illusion. By making his characters 'actors' in
their own world, Jonson goes further, creating overlapping layers of
illusion and reflecting the deceptions of Volpone's Venice in the
play's very form. Throughout Act One Volpone remains in his bed,

pretending to be insensible to the scavengers' visits. The bed becomes a stage within the stage, and Volpone's 'act' constitutes the kind of play within a play so beloved of Renaissance audiences. The play's whole world is a kind of theatre, with its own actors, stories and playing spaces – and with an 'audience' tricked into believing that its deceptions are true.

Renaissance Venice

The play's setting is crucial to the whole balance between illusion and reality. The Venice of the Renaissance had long been the most prosperous centre of trade in the Christian world: positioned at the edge of known Europe, it was the conduit through which the goods of Asia and Arabia flowed. Founded upon mercantalism and possessing great wealth, it was perceived abroad as the seat both of materialism triumphant and of the corruption which was its inevitable consequence. When, for example, Iago in *Othello* plans to turn his master's mind to jealousy, he speaks of the 'super-subtle' Venetians, reiterating the commonly held belief that the inhabitants of that city were masters of duplicity. We see a similar view of Venice in *Volpone*, in its inhabitants' remorseless pursuit of riches and the plots and dissemblings upon which they embark. The idea of a society corrupted by acquisitiveness is augmented by the imagery of disease that runs through the play. Volpone's own feigned malady and others' lurid descriptions of its symptoms, his disguise as a mountebank physician, the details of various elixirs and remedies – with these the 'sickness' that lies at the heart of Venice is symbolised in the corrupt bodies of its citizens.

Such corruption ultimately threatens the very fabric of Venetian society. As a result of Volpone's intrigues, Voltore, an advocate, perjures himself in court, betraying the principle of justice which he is supposed to hold dear. Family relationships are undermined: Corbaccio disinherits his son, Bonario, while Corvino willingly ushers his own wife, Celia, into Volpone's arms. As the crucial legal and familial relationships of society are themselves destroyed, the dark side of Venice's corruption, and of Volpone's intrigues, becomes apparent.

The Trial Scene

Corruption reaches its climax in Act IV, Scene v. Having overheard Volpone's attempted seduction of Celia, Bonario rescues her from his embrace, and the pair then charge the Fox and his would-be heirs with their crimes, summoning them before the Venetian court. But then, in a remarkable dramatic set-piece, truth is turned on its head. Calling as witnesses all the plotters and dissemblers, the advocate Voltore argues that it is Bonario and Celia who are guilty; they are, he says, lovers, plotting to steal Corbaccio's money, and in the process slandering the names of their guiltless fellow Venetians. His speech culminates with Volpone himself appearing before the court as an invalid, Voltore ironically greeting his entrance with 'here's the ravisher / The rider on men's wives, the great imposter / The grand voluptuary.' Volpone is of course all these things, but by speaking with such apparent irony, Voltore convinces the court that the opposite is true. All goodness has been made to seem wicked and all wickedness good; the corruption of Venice is completed in a total inversion of truth, and the play's only honest characters, Bonario and Celia, are led away to await punishment.

The trial scene is equally remarkable for the strands of deception it weaves together. In order to ensure the scavengers' compliance in this grand act of misrepresentation, Mosca has told each of them a different story; each believes the lie is being told for their benefit, and ultimately only Mosca and the audience know the truth. Like Volpone's 'act' as the bedridden invalid, the trial scene is a piece of theatre, staged within the world of Venice and 'directed' by Mosca, who now reveals himself to be the greatest dissembler of all. Even so, there have been indications of this all along. It is Mosca who actually manages Volpone's intrigues; pretending to be working in the best interests of Voltore, Corbaccio, Corvino and Lady Would-be in turn, he presents a different face to each, and in doing so prompts all to part with their riches. In Act III, Scene i, he explains, expounding on the noble profession of the toadying servant or 'parasite'. The parasite, he argues, is not a base individual, for it is a role which demands extra-ordinary grace and agility of mind, the ability to 'Shoot through the air as nimbly as a star; / Turn short as does a swallow . . . Present to any humour all occasion:/ And change a visor swifter than a thought.'

All this being so, it is perhaps no surprise that the face Mosca presents to Volpone, the persona of the loyal servant, proves as false as all the others. Once more facing the Venetian court, but this time after the news of his own 'death' has been spread abroad, Volpone is trapped in the disguise of a Commendatore that he has adopted. Mosca agrees to free him, to assert that his master is indeed alive, only on condition that he be granted half – and, later, all – the Fox's fortune. Faced with a whipping and the loss of his riches, Volpone has however little left to lose, and, throwing off his disguise, he reveals all their machinations, condemning himself and Mosca, as well as the scavengers, to their respective fates. In this way, just as Volpone over-reached himself by embarking upon ever more precarious intrigues, so Mosca's ambition has proved his own undoing, and their punishment reestablishes the moral order of the world.

The English Renaissance and its Theatre

The Renaissance in Britain was a time of massive change and growth. In the sixteenth and seventeenth centuries a series of bad harvests and market fluctuations irreparably damaged the old land-based economy by bankrupting smallholders, whose lands were then gathered up into larger estates. One result of this was a steady migration from the country into the towns; it is estimated that in the 1580s London had a population of approximately fifty thousand, whereas a hundred years later it was in excess of half a million. The city in which Jonson's plays were performed was a fast-expanding, crowded place, with a pace of life far more frenetic than that of the countryside where many of its new inhabitants would have been born.

The Renaissance was also a time of exploration, with English traders and colonisers venturing into Asia, Africa and the New World, returning to their homeland and establishing London as a world centre of commerce. The new mercantilism affected all levels of life: the rich were richer than ever, and the poor poorer. This would have been particularly evident in a choked metropolis such as London, where different social classes were not yet separated into different communal areas, and the 'high' rubbed shoulders with the 'low' on a daily basis. The audience for *Volpone* would have comprised not

only lords and ladies, but also the professional and trading classes –
the so-called citizens or 'cits' – as well as those of the working class
affluent enough to afford the price of admission. For Londoners of
the seventeenth century, the play's central image of a society based
on materialist values would not have been abstract but directly
relevant to their lives.

In their own day writers like Jonson and Shakespeare had nothing
like the status they do today. Creating theatre, or even attending it,
was considered a morally dubious pastime. From the Middle Ages
there stemmed a tradition of the Devil as '*fals semblant*', the one who
adopts pleasing disguises to lure souls into damnation. In the
sixteenth century Elizabeth I introduced laws forbidding her subjects
to wear clothes deemed unsuitable to their social class. Pretending to
be someone else was an activity viewed with mistrust in Renaissance
England – and one consequence was that play performances were
banned within the confines of the City of London itself. As a result
theatres congregated in areas such as Shoreditch and the South Bank
of the River Thames, beyond the city walls. Plays were performed
alongside such other 'suspect' activities as prostitution, cockfighting
and bear-baiting – indeed, companies sometimes employed the same
venues, and drama was not considered an art form but a form of
entertainment. Jonson was the first English playwright to publish his
writing under the title *Works*, an action which caused raised eyebrows,
since at the time 'works' was an evocative word, usually reserved for
'higher' forms such as treatises on philosophy or theology.

Volpone was first performed in 1605 or 1606 in the university towns of
Oxford and Cambridge by one of London's leading companies, the
King's Men, but was restaged regularly throughout the seventeenth
century. In the Renaissance plays such as Jonson's were performed in
surroundings quite different from those we are familiar with today.
The purpose-built theatres of the time typically consisted of a round
– or, more accurately, polygonal – structure into which were built
perhaps three storeys of seating for the audience. Other spectators
would stand in the pit area surrounding the thrust stage: the entry fee
to this area was the cheapest, and this section of the audience
Shakespeare referred to as the 'groundlings'. The stage – a raised,
square dais, topped with a roof – projected into the theatre's central

well, while above it and to the rear ran a balcony. This architectural arrangement offered the Renaissance theatre company a variety of areas in which to stage the action. After around 1609, some adult companies began playing also in indoor or 'private' theatres, previously used only by children's companies. Here, a smaller capacity and higher prices made for more socially select audiences.

The Renaissance stage employed only the barest of sets. A table thrust onstage was enough to indicate a banqueting room, a bed a bedroom. Scenes were often conjured up in a character's lines. Costumes, however, were often sumptuous and were sometimes 'real' clothes, it being the custom for companies to buy items at a reduced price from people who had no more use for them, or to be left the wardrobe of a noble patron.

Colin Counsell

For Further Reading

Of the critical works on Jonson now available, J.A. Barish, *Ben Jonson and the Language of Prose Comedy* (Harvard University Press, 1960), and A. Barton, *Ben Jonson, Dramatist* (Cambridge University Press, 1984), are interesting and accessible, while Brian Gibbons's *Jacobean City Comedy* (Methuen, 1980), relates Jonson's work to that of other dramatists of the period. Good details of the theatre of the time are given in Volume III of *The Revels History of Drama in English* (Methuen, 1975), and J.L. Styan *Shakespeare's Stagecraft* (Cambridge University Press, 1967). D.J. Palmer (ed.), *Comedy: Developments in Criticism* (Macmillan, 1984), although heavily theoretical and sometimes contentious, does contain relevant writings by Sir Philip Sidney and by Jonson himself.

Jonson: Key Dates

1572 Benjamin Jonson born in London.

1594 Jonson marries.

1597 Jonson is commissioned by Henslowe to complete Thomas
      Nashe's unfinished play *The Isle of Dogs*. The finished work is
      judged seditious and Jonson, along with several of the
      company, is imprisoned.

1598 Jonson writes the successful *Every Man in His Humour*, per-
      formed by the Lord Chamberlain's company with William
      Shakespeare in the cast. Jonson kills the actor Gabriel Spencer
      in a duel, and is imprisoned.

1599-1614
      The period of Jonson's great comic masterpieces.

1605 Jonson joins with John Marston and George Chapman to
      write *Eastward Ho!*: the play offends James I, and Jonson and
      Marston are imprisoned. Jonson writes *The Masque of
      Blacknesse*, the first of his court masques. Thereafter masques
      formed a main part of his output.

1616 Jonson publishes his *Works*.

1631 Jonson and Inigo Jones, designer of the court masques,
      quarrel. They never again work together.

1637 Jonson dies and is buried in Westminster Abbey, his tomb-
      stone bearing the legend 'O rare Ben Jonson'.

VOLPONE

TO THE MOST NOBLE AND MOST EQUAL SISTERS,
THE TWO FAMOUS UNIVERSITIES, FOR THEIR LOVE AND
ACCEPTANCE SHOWN TO HIS POEM IN THE PRESENTATION,
BEN. JONSON, THE GRATEFUL ACKNOWLEDGER,
DEDICATES BOTH IT AND HIMSELF

The Persons of the Play

VOLPONE, *a Magnifico.*
MOSCA, *his Parasite.*
VOLTORE, *an Advocate.*
CORBACCIO, *an old Gentleman.*
CORVINO, *a Merchant.*
NANO, *a Dwarf.*
CASTRONE, *an Eunuch.*
ANDROGYNO, *a[n] Hermaphrodite.*
[SIR] POLITIC WOULD-BE, *a[n English] Knight.*
PEREGRINE, *a[n English] Gent[leman]-traveller.*
BONARIO, *a young Gentleman [, son to Corbaccio].*
FINE MADA[ME] WOULD-BE, *the Knight's wife.*
CELIA, *the Merchant's wife.*
AVOCATORI, *Four Magistrates.*
NOTARIO, *the Register.*
COMMANDATORI, *Officers [of justice].*
MERCATORI, *three Merchants.*
SERVITOR[I], *Servant[s].*
GREGE [, *a Crowd*].
WOMEN, *two [Attendants on Lady Would-be].*

The scene: Venice.

The Argument

V OLPONE, childless, rich, feigns sick, despairs,
O ffers his state to hopes of several heirs,
L ies languishing; his Parasite receives
P resents of all, assures, deludes; then weaves
O ther Gross plots, which ope themselves, are told.   5
N ew tricks for safety are sought; they thrive: when, bold
E ach tempts th'other again, and all are sold.

Prologue

Now, luck yet send us, and a little wit
    Will serve to make our play hit,
According to the palates of the season;
    Here is rhyme not empty of reason:
This we were bid to credit from our poet,   5
    Whose true scope, if you would know it,
In all his poems still hath been this measure:
    To mix profit with your pleasure;
And not as some, whose throats their envy failing,
    Cry hoarsely, 'All he writes is railing',   10
And, when his plays come forth, think they can flout them
    With saying, 'He was a year about them'.
To these there needs no lie but this his creature,
    Which was, two months since, no feature;
And though he dares give them five lives to mend it,   15
    'Tis known, five weeks fully penned it,
From his own hand, without a coadjutor,
    Novice, journeyman, or tutor.

Yet thus much I can give you as a token
   Of his play's worth: no eggs are broken,   20
Nor quaking custards with fierce teeth affrighted,
   Wherewith your rout are so delighted;
Nor hales he in a gull, old ends reciting,
   To stop gaps in his loose writing;
With such a deal of monstrous and forced action,   25
   As might make Bedlam a faction;
Nor made he his play for jests stol'n from each table,
   But makes jests to fit his fable.
And so presents quick comedy refined,
   As best critics have designed;   30
The laws of Time, Place, Persons he observeth,
   From no needful rule he swerveth.
All gall and copperas from his ink he draineth,
   Only a little salt remaineth,
Wherewith he'll rub your cheeks, till, red with laughter,   35
   They shall look fresh a week after.

Act I, Scene i

[*Enter*] MOSCA [*and discovers*] VOLPONE [*in his bed*].

[VOLPONE.] [*Rising.*] Good morning to the day; and next, my gold!
    Open the shrine that I may see my saint.

[MOSCA *draws a curtain to disclose* VOLPONE*'s treasure.*]

Hail, the world's soul, and mine! More glad than is
The teeming earth to see the longed-for sun
Peep through the horns of the celestial Ram,   5
Am I, to view thy splendour, darkening his;
That, lying here amongst my other hoards,
Show'st like a flame by night, or like the day
Struck out of chaos, when all darkness fled
Unto the centre. O thou son of Sol,   10
But brighter than thy father, let me kiss,
With adoration, thee, and every relic
Of sacred treasure in this blessed room.
Well did wise poets by thy glorious name
Title that age which they would have the best,   15
Thou being the best of things, and far transcending
All style of joy in children, parents, friends,
Or any other waking dream on earth.
Thy looks when they to Venus did ascribe,
They should have giv'n her twenty thousand cupids,   20
Such are thy beauties and our loves! Dear saint,
Riches, the dumb god that givest all men tongues,
That canst do nought and yet makest men do all things;
The price of souls; even hell, with thee to boot,
Is made worth heaven! Thou art virtue, fame,   25
Honour, and all things else! Who can get thee,
He shall be noble, valiant, honest, wise –

MOSCA. And what he will, sir. Riches are in fortune
   A greater good than wisdom is in nature.

VOLPONE. True my beloved Mosca. Yet I glory   30
   More in the cunning purchase of my wealth
   Than in the glad possession, since I gain
   No common way: I use no trade, no venture;
   I wound no earth with ploughshares; fat no beasts
   To feed the shambles; have no mills for iron,   35
   Oil, corn, or men, to grind 'em into powder;
   I blow no subtle glass; expose no ships
   To threat'nings of the furrow-faced sea;
   I turn no monies in the public bank
   Nor usure private –

MOSCA.   No, sir, nor devour   40
   Soft prodigals. You shall ha' some will swallow
   A melting heir as glibly as your Dutch
   Will pills of butter, and ne'er purge for 't;
   Tear forth the fathers of poor families
   Out of their beds, and coffin them, alive,   45
   In some kind, clasping prison, where their bones
   May be forthcoming when the flesh is rotten:
   But your sweet nature doth abhor these courses;
   You loathe the widow's or the orphan's tears
   Should wash your pavements, or their piteous cries 50
   Ring in your roofs and beat the air for vengeance –

VOLPONE. Right, Mosca, I do loathe it.

MOSCA.   And besides, sir,
   You are not like the thresher that doth stand
   With a huge flail, watching a heap of corn,
   And, hungry, dares not taste the smallest grain,   55
   But feeds on mallows and such bitter herbs;
   Nor like the merchant who hath filled his vaults
   With *Romagnia* and rich Candian wines,
   Yet drinks the lees of Lombard's vinegar.
   You will not lie in straw whilst moths and worms 60
   Feed on your sumptuous hangings and soft beds.

You know the use of riches, and dare give, now,
From that bright heap, to me, your poor observer,
Or to your dwarf, or your hermaphrodite,
Your eunuch, or what other household trifle   65
Your pleasure allows maintenance –

VOLPONE.   Hold thee, Mosca,
Take of my hand. [*Gives him money.*] Thou strikest on truth in all,
And they are envious term thee parasite.
Call forth my dwarf, my eunuch, and my fool,
And let 'em make me sport.

[*Exit* MOSCA.]
                                        What should I do   70
But cocker up my genius and live free
To all delights my fortune calls me to?
I have no wife, no parent, child, ally,
To give my substance to; but whom I make
Must be my heir: and this makes men observe me.   75
This draws new clients, daily, to my house,
Women and men, of every sex and age,
That bring me presents, send me plate, coin, jewels,
With hope that when I die (which they expect
Each greedy minute) it shall then return   80
Tenfold upon them; whilst some, covetous
Above the rest, seek to engross me whole,
And counter-work the one unto the other,
Contend in gifts, as they would seem in love:
All which I suffer, playing with their hopes,   85
And am content to coin 'em into profit,
And look upon their kindness, and take more,
And look on that; still bearing them in hand,
Letting the cherry knock against their lips,
And draw it by their mouths, and back again. –   90
How now!

Act I, Scene ii

NANO, ANDROGYNO, [*and*] CASTRONE [*enter, to entertain*]
VOLPONE, MOSCA [*following them*].

[NANO.] Now, room for fresh gamesters, who do will you to know,
    They do bring you neither play nor university show;
And therefore do entreat you that whatsoever they rehearse
    May not fare a whit the worse for the false pace of the verse.
If you wonder at this, you will wonder more ere we pass,   5
    For know, here [*Indicating* ANDROGYNO.] is enclosed the
        soul of Pythagoras,
That juggler divine, as hereafter shall follow;
    Which soul, fast and loose, sir, came first from Apollo,
And was breathed into Aethalides, Mercurius his son,
    Where it had the gift to remember all that ever was done.   10
From thence it fled forth, and made quick transmigration
    To goldilocked Euphorbus, who was killed in good fashion
At the siege of old Troy by the cuckold of Sparta.
    Hermotimus was next (I find it in my charta)
To whom it did pass, where no sooner it was missing   15
    But with one Pyrrhus of Delos it learned to go a-fishing;
And thence did it enter the sophist of Greece.
    From Pythagore, she went into a beautiful piece
Hight Aspasia, the *meretrix*; and the next toss of her
    Was again of a whore she became a philosopher,   20
Crates the cynic – as itself doth relate it;
    Since, kings, knights, and beggars, knaves, lords, and fools gat it,
Besides ox and ass, camel, mule, goat, and brock,
    In all which it hath spoke as in the cobbler's cock.
But I come not here to discourse of that matter,   25
    Or his one, two, or three, or his great oath, 'By *quater*!'
His musics, his *trigon*, his golden thigh,
    Or his telling how elements shift; but I
Would ask how of late thou hast suffered translation,
    And shifted thy coat in these days of reformation?   30

ANDROGYNO. Like one of the reformed, a fool, as you see,
    Counting all old doctrine heresy.

NANO. But not on thine own forbid meats hast thou ventured?

ANDROGYNO. On fish, when first a Carthusian I entered.

NANO. Why, then thy dogmatical silence hath left thee?   35

ANDROGYNO. Of that an obstreperous lawyer bereft me.

NANO. O wonderful change! When sir lawyer forsook thee,
          For Pythagore's sake, what body then took thee?

ANDROGYNO. A good dull mule.

NANO.   And how, by that means,
          Thou wert brought to allow of the eating of beans?   40

ANDROGYNO. Yes.

NANO.   But from the mule into whom didst thou pass?

ANDROGYNO. Into a very strange beast, by some writers called an
               ass;
          By others a precise, pure, illuminate brother
     Of those devour flesh, and sometimes one another,
          And will drop you forth a libel, or a sanctified lie,   45
     Betwixt every spoonful of a Nativity pie.

NANO. Now quit thee, for heaven, of that profane nation,
          And gently report thy next transmigration.

ANDROGYNO. To the same that I am.

NANO.   A creature of delight,
          And what is more than a fool, an hermaphrodite?   50
     Now, pray thee, sweet soul, in all thy variation,
          Which body wouldst thou choose to take up thy station?

ANDROGYNO. Troth, this I am in, even here would I tarry.

NANO. 'Cause here the delight of each sex thou canst vary?

ANDROGYNO. Alas, those pleasures be stale and forsaken;   55
          No, 'tis your fool wherewith I am so taken,
     The only one creature that I can call blessed,
          For all other forms I have proved most distressed.

NANO. Spoke true, as thou wert in Pythagoras still.
    This learned opinion we celebrate will,   60
  Fellow eunuch, as behooves us, with all our wit and art,
      To dignify that whereof ourselves are so great and special a
        part.

VOLPONE. Now, very, very pretty! Mosca, this
  Was thy invention?

MOSCA.   If it please my patron,
  Not else.

VOLPONE. It doth, good Mosca.

MOSCA.   Then it was, sir.   65

    [NANO *and* CASTRONE *sing.*]

SONG.
  Fools, they are the only nation
  Worth men's envy or admiration;
  Free from care or sorrow-taking,
  Selves and others merry making:
  All they speak or do is sterling.   70
  Your fool he is your great man's dearling,
  And your lady's sport and pleasure;
  Tongue and bauble are his treasure.
  E'en his face begetteth laughter,
  And he speaks truth free from slaughter;   75
  He's the grace of every feast,
  And, sometimes, the chiefest guest;
  Hath his trencher and his stool
  When wit waits upon the fool.
  O, who would not be   80
  He, he, he?

One knocks without.

VOLPONE. Who's that? Away! [*Exeunt* NANO *and* CASTRONE.]
                Look, Mosca.

MOSCA.   Fool, begone!

[*Exit* ANDROGYNO.]

'Tis Signor Voltore, the advocate;
I know him by his knock.

VOLPONE.   Fetch me my gown,
My furs, and night-caps. Say my couch is changing,   85
And let him entertain himself awhile
Without i' th' gallery.

[*Exit* MOSCA.]

                    Now, now, my clients
Begin their visitation! Vulture, kite,
Raven, and gorcrow, all my birds of prey
That think me turning carcass, now they come;   90
I am not for 'em yet.

[*Re-enter* MOSCA, *with the gown, etc.*]

How now? the news?

MOSCA. [*Helping him dress.*] A piece of plate, sir.

VOLPONE.   Of what bigness?

MOSCA.   Huge,
Massy, and antique, with your name inscribed
And arms engraven.

VOLPONE.   Good! – and not a fox
Stretched on the earth, with fine delusive sleights,   95
Mocking a gaping crow? ha, Mosca!

MOSCA. [*Laughing.*]   Sharp, sir.

VOLPONE. Give me my furs. Why dost thou laugh so, man?

MOSCA. I cannot choose, sir, when I apprehend
What thoughts he has without now, as he walks:
That this might be the last gift he should give;   100
That this would fetch you; if you died today,
And gave him all, what he should be tomorrow;
What large return would come of all his ventures;
How he should worshipped be, and reverenced;

Ride with his furs and foot-cloths; waited on   105
By herds of fools and clients; have clear way
Made for his mule, as lettered as himself;
Be called the great and learned advocate:
And then concludes, there's nought impossible.   109

VOLPONE. [*Climbing into bed.*] Yes, to be learned, Mosca.

MOSCA.   O, no: rich
Implies it. Hood an ass with reverend purple,
So you can hide his two ambitious ears,
And he shall pass for a cathedral doctor.

VOLPONE. My caps, my caps, good Mosca. Fetch him in.

MOSCA. Stay, sir; your ointment for your eyes.

VOLPONE.   That's true;   115
Dispatch, dispatch! I long to have possession
Of my new present.

MOSCA. [*Anointing* VOLPONE's *eyes.*] That, and thousands more,
I hope to see you lord of.

VOLPONE.   Thanks, kind Mosca.

MOSCA. And that, when I am lost in blended dust,
And hundred such as I am in succession, –   120

VOLPONE. Nay, that were too much, Mosca.

MOSCA.   You shall live
Still to delude these harpies.

VOLPONE.   Loving Mosca! [*Looking into a mirror.*]
'Tis well. My pillow now, and let him enter.

[*Exit* MOSCA.]

Now, my feigned cough, my phthisic, and my gout,
My apoplexy, palsy, and catarrhs,   125
Help, with your forced functions, this my posture,
Wherein this three year I have milked their hopes.
He comes; I hear him [*He coughs.*] Uh! uh! uh! uh! O –

Act I, Scene iii

[*Enter to him*] MOSCA [*with*] VOLTORE.

[MOSCA.] [*To* VOLTORE.] You still are what you were, sir.
>   Only you,
> Of all the rest, are he commands his love;
> And you do wisely to preserve it thus
> With early visitation, and kind notes
> Of your good meaning to him, which, I know,   5
> Cannot but come most grateful. [*To* VOLPONE.] Patron! Sir!
> Here's Signor Voltore is come –

VOLPONE. [*Faintly.*]   What say you?

MOSCA. Sir, Signor Voltore is come this morning
> To visit you.

VOLPONE.   I thank him.

MOSCA.   And hath brought
> A piece of antique plate, bought of St Mark,   10
> With which he here presents you.

VOLPONE.   He is welcome.
> Pray him to come more often.

MOSCA.   Yes.

VOLTORE.   What says he?

MOSCA. He thanks you and desires you see him often.

VOLPONE. Mosca.

MOSCA.   My patron?

VOLPONE.   Bring him near. Where is he?
> I long to feel his hand.

MOSCA. [*Prompting* VOLTORE.] The plate is here, sir.   15

VOLTORE. How fare you, sir?

VOLPONE.   I thank you, Signor Voltore.
> Where is the plate? Mine eyes are bad.

VOLTORE. [*Puts it into his grasp.*]   I'm sorry
  To see you still thus weak.

MOSCA. [*Aside.*]   That he is not weaker.

VOLPONE. You are too munificent.

VOLTORE.   No, sir; would to heaven
  I could as well give health to you as that plate.   20

VOLPONE. You give, sir, what you can. I thank you. Your love
  Hath taste in this, and shall not be unanswered.
  I pray you see me often.

VOLTORE.   Yes, I shall, sir.

VOLPONE. Be not far from me.

MOSCA. [*To* VOLTORE.]   Do you observe that, sir?

VOLPONE. Hearken unto me still; it will concern you.   25

MOSCA. You are a happy man, sir; know your good.

VOLPONE. I cannot now last long –

MOSCA. [*Whispering, aside.*]   You are his heir, sir.

VOLTORE. Am I?

VOLPONE.   I feel me going – uh! uh! uh! uh! –
  I am sailing to my port – uh! uh! uh! uh! –
  And I am glad I am so near my haven.   30

MOSCA. Alas, kind gentleman. Well, we must all go –

VOLTORE. But Mosca –

MOSCA.   Age will conquer.

VOLTORE.   Pray thee, hear me.
  Am I inscribed his heir for certain?

MOSCA.   Are you?
  I do beseech you, sir, you will vouchsafe
  To write me in your family. All my hopes   35
  Depend upon your worship. I am lost
  Except the rising sun do shine on me.

VOLTORE. It shall both shine and warm thee, Mosca.

MOSCA.   Sir,
    I am a man that have not done your love
    All the worst offices. Here I wear your keys,   40
    See all your coffers and your caskets locked,
    Keep the poor inventory of your jewels,
    Your plate, and moneys, am your steward, sir,
    Husband your goods here.

VOLTORE.   But am I sole heir?

MOSCA. Without a partner, sir, confirmed this morning;   45
    The wax is warm yet, and the ink scarce dry
    Upon the parchment.

VOLTORE.   Happy, happy me!
    By what good chance, sweet Mosca?

MOSCA.   Your desert, sir;
    I know no second cause.

VOLTORE.   Thy modesty
    Is loath to know it; well, we shall requite it.   50

MOSCA. He ever liked your course, sir; that first took him.
    I oft have heard him say how he admired
    Men of your large profession, that could speak
    To every cause, and things mere contraries,
    Till they were hoarse again, yet all be law;   55
    That, with most quick agility, could turn,
    And re-turn; make knots, and undo them;
    Give forked counsel; take provoking gold
    On either hand, and put it up: these men,
    He knew, would thrive with their humility.   60
    And, for his part, he thought he should be blessed
    To have his heir of such a suffering spirit,
    So wise, so grave, of so perplexed a tongue,
    And loud withal, that would not wag, nor scarce
    Lie still, without a fee; when every word   65
    Your worship but lets fall is a *chequin*!

Another knocks.

Who's that? One knocks. I would not have you seen, sir
And yet – pretend you came and went in haste;
I'll fashion an excuse. And, gentle sir,
When you do come to swim in golden lard,   70
Up to the arms in honey, that your chin
Is borne up stiff with fatness of the flood,
Think on your vassal; but remember me:
I ha' not been your worst of clients.

VOLTORE.   Mosca –

MOSCA. When will you have your inventory brought, sir?   75
Or see a copy of the will? [*Knock repeated.*] Anon!
[*To* VOLTORE.] I'll bring 'em to you, sir. Away, begone;
Put business i' your face.

[*Exit* VOLTORE.]

VOLPONE. [*Springing up.*]   Excellent, Mosca!
Come hither, let me kiss thee.

MOSCA.   Keep you still, sir.
Here is Corbaccio.

VOLPONE.   Set the plate away.   80
The vulture's gone, and the old raven's come.

Act I, Scene iv

[MOSCA.] Betake you to your silence and your sleep.
[*He puts the plate away.*] Stand there and multiply. Now we shall see
A wretch who is indeed more impotent
Than this can feign to be, yet hopes to hop
Over his grave.

[*Enter to them* CORBACCIO.]

                  Signor Corbaccio!   5
You're very welcome, sir.

CORBACCIO.   How does your patron?

MOSCA. Troth, as he did, sir; no amends.

CORBACCIO. [*Mishearing.*]   What! mends he?

MOSCA. [*Loudly.*] No, sir: he is rather worse.

CORBACCIO.   That's well.
  Where is he?

MOSCA. Upon his couch, sir, newly fall'n asleep.

CORBACCIO. Does he sleep well?

MOSCA.   No wink, sir, all this night,   10
  Nor yesterday; but slumbers.

CORBACCIO. Good! He should take
  Some counsel of physicians. I have brought him
  An opiate here from mine own doctor –

MOSCA. He will not hear of drugs.

CORBACCIO.   Why? I myself
  Stood by while 't was made, saw all th'ingredients,   15
  And know it cannot but most gently work.
  My life for his, 'tis but to make him sleep.

VOLPONE. [*Aside.*] Ay, his last sleep, if he would take it.

MOSCA.   Sir,
  He has no faith in physic.

CORBACCIO.   Say you? Say you?

MOSCA. He has no faith in physic. He does think   20
  Most of your doctors are the greater danger,
  And worse disease t'escape. I often have
  Heard him protest that your physician
  Should never be his heir.

CORBACCIO.   Not I his heir?

MOSCA. Not your physician, sir.

CORBACCIO.   O, no, no, no,   25

I do not mean it.

MOSCA.   No, sir, nor their fees
He cannot brook; he says they flay a man
Before they kill him.

CORBACCIO.   Right, I do conceive you.

MOSCA. And then, they do it by experiment,
For which the law not only doth absolve 'em,   30
But gives them great reward; and he is loath
To hire his death so.

CORBACCIO.   It is true, they kill
With as much licence as a judge.

MOSCA.   Nay, more;
For he but kills, sir, where the law condemns,
And these can kill him too.

CORBACCIO.   Ay, or me,   35
Or any man. How does his apoplex?
Is that strong on him still?

MOSCA.   Most violent.
His speech is broken, and his eyes are set,
His face drawn longer than 't was wont –

CORBACCIO.   How? how?
Stronger than he was wont?

MOSCA.   No, sir; his face   40
Drawn longer than 't was wont.

CORBACCIO.   O, good!

MOSCA.   His mouth
Is ever gaping, and his eyelids hang.

CORBACCIO.   Good.

MOSCA. A freezing numbness stiffens all his joints,
And makes the colour of his flesh like lead.

CORBACCIO.   'Tis good.

MOSCA. His pulse beats slow and dull.

CORBACCIO. Good symptoms still. 45

MOSCA. And from his brain –

CORBACCIO. Ha! how? not from his brain?

MOSCA. Yes, sir, and from his brain –

CORBACCIO. I conceive you; good.

MOSCA. Flows a cold sweat, with a continual rheum
   Forth the resolved corners of his eyes.

CORBACCIO. Is't possible? Yet I am better, ha! 50
   How does he with the swimming of his head?

MOSCA. O, sir, 'tis past the scotomy; he now
   Hath lost his feeling, and hath left to snort;
   You hardly can perceive him that he breathes.

CORBACCIO. Excellent, excellent; sure I shall outlast him! 55
   This makes me young again, a score of years.

MOSCA. I was a-coming for you, sir.

CORBACCIO. Has he made his will;
   What has he given me?

MOSCA. No, sir.

CORBACCIO. Nothing? ha!

MOSCA. He has not made his will, sir.

CORBACCIO. O, O, O.
   What then did Voltore, the lawyer, here? 60

MOSCA. He smelled a carcass, sir, when he but heard
   My master was about his testament;
   As I did urge him to it for your good –

CORBACCIO. He came unto him, did he? I thought so.

MOSCA. Yes, and presented him this piece of plate. 65

CORBACCIO. To be his heir?

MOSCA.   I do not know, sir.

CORBACCIO.   True,
  I know it too.

MOSCA. [*Aside.*] By your own scale, sir.

CORBACCIO.   Well,
  I shall prevent him yet. See, Mosca, look:
  Here I have brought a bag of bright *chequins*
  Will quite weigh down his plate.

MOSCA. [*Taking the bag.*]   Yea, marry, sir!   70
  This is true physic, this your sacred medicine;
  No talk of opiates to this great elixir.

CORBACCIO. 'Tis *aurum palpabile*, if not *potabile*.

MOSCA. It shall be ministered to him in his bowl?

CORBACCIO. Ay, do, do, do.

MOSCA.   Most blessed cordial!   75
  This will recover him.

CORBACCIO.   Yes, do, do, do.

MOSCA. I think it were not best, sir.

CORBACCIO.   What?

MOSCA.   To recover him.

CORBACCIO. O, no, no, no; by no means.

MOSCA.   Why, sir, this
  Will work some strange effect if he but feel it.

CORBACCIO. 'Tis true, therefore forbear; I'll take my venture;   80
  Give me 't again.

MOSCA.   At no hand. Pardon me.
  You shall not do yourself that wrong, sir. I
  Will so advise you, you shall have it all.

CORBACCIO. How!

MOSCA.   All, sir; 'tis your right, your own; no man

Can claim a part; 'tis yours without a rival,   85
    Decreed by destiny.

CORBACCIO.   How? How, good Mosca?

MOSCA. I'll tell you, sir. This fit he shall recover –

CORBACCIO. I do conceive you.

MOSCA.   And, on first advantage
    Of his gained sense, will I re-importune him
    Unto the making of his testament,   90
    And show him this. [*He points to the money.*]

CORBACCIO.   Good, good.

MOSCA.   'Tis better yet,
    If you will hear sir.

CORBACCIO.   Yes, with all my heart.

MOSCA. Now would I counsel you, make home with speed;
    There, frame a will whereto you shall inscribe
    My master your sole heir.

CORBACCIO.   And disinherit   95
    My son?

MOSCA.   O, sir, the better; for that colour
    Shall make it much more taking.

CORBACCIO.   O, but colour?

MOSCA. This will, sir, you shall send it unto me.
    Now, when I come to enforce, as I will do,
    Your cares, your watchings, and your many prayers,   100
    Your more than many gifts, your this day's present,
    And last, produce your will; where, without thought
    Or least regard unto your proper issue,
    A son so brave and highly meriting,
    The stream of your diverted love hath thrown you   105
    Upon my master, and made him your heir;
    He cannot be so stupid, or stone dead,
    But out of conscience and mere gratitude –

CORBACCIO. He must pronounce me his?

MOSCA.   'Tis true.

CORBACCIO.   This plot
  Did I think on before.

MOSCA.   I do believe it.   110

CORBACCIO. Do you not believe it?

MOSCA.   Yes, sir.

CORBACCIO.   Mine own project.

MOSCA. Which, when he hath done, sir –

CORBACCIO.   Published me his heir?

MOSCA. And you so certain to survive him –

CORBACCIO.   Ay.

MOSCA. Being so lusty a man –

CORBACCIO.   'Tis true.

MOSCA.   Yes, sir –

CORBACCIO. I thought on that too. See, how he should be   115
  The very organ to express my thoughts!

MOSCA. You have not only done yourself a good –

CORBACCIO. But multiplied it on my son?

MOSCA.   'Tis right, sir.

CORBACCIO. Still my invention.

MOSCA.   'Las, sir, heaven knows
  It hath been all my study, all my care,   120
  (I e'en grow grey withal) how to work things –

CORBACCIO. I do conceive, sweet Mosca.

MOSCA.   You are he
  For whom I labour here.

CORBACCIO.   Ay, do, do, do.

I'll straight about it. [*Going.*]

MOSCA. [*Aside.*]   Rook go with you, raven!

CORBACCIO. I know thee honest.

MOSCA. [*Aside.*]   You do lie, sir –

CORBACCIO.   And –   125

MOSCA. [*Aside.*] Your knowledge is no better than your ears, sir.

CORBACCIO. I do not doubt to be a father to thee.

MOSCA. [*Aside.*] Nor I to gull my brother of his blessing.

CORBACCIO. I may ha' my youth restored to me, why not?   129

MOSCA. [*Aside.*] Your worship is a precious ass –

CORBACCIO.   What sayst thou?

MOSCA. I do desire your worship to make haste, sir.

CORBACCIO. 'Tis done, 'tis done; I go. [*Exit.*]

VOLPONE. [*Leaping from his couch.*]   O, I shall burst!
    Let out my sides, let out my sides –

MOSCA.   Contain
    Your flux of laughter, sir. You know this hope
    Is such a bait it covers any hook.   135

VOLPONE. O, but thy working and thy placing it!
    I cannot hold; good rascal, let me kiss thee.

    [*Embraces him.*]

    I never knew thee in so rare a humour.

MOSCA. Alas, sir, I but do as I am taught;
    Follow your grave instructions; give 'em words;   140
    Pour oil into their ears, and send them hence.

VOLPONE. 'Tis true, 'tis true. What a rare punishment
    Is avarice to itself!

MOSCA.   Ay, with our help, sir.

VOLPONE. So many cares, so many maladies,
   So many fears attending on old age;   145
   Yea, death so often called on, as no wish
   Can be more frequent with 'em. Their limbs faint,
   Their senses dull, their seeing, hearing, going,
   All dead before them; yea, their very teeth,
   Their instruments of eating, failing them: 150
   Yet this is reckoned life! Nay, here was one
   Is now gone home, that wishes to live longer!
   Feels not his gout, nor palsy; feigns himself
   Younger by scores of years; flatters his age
   With confident belying it; hopes he may   155
   With charms, like Aeson, have his youth restored;
   And with these thoughts so battens, as if fate
   Would be as easily cheated on as he,
   And all turns air!

Another knocks.

                 Who's that there, now? a third?

MOSCA. Close, to your couch again; I hear his voice.   160
   It is Corvino, our spruce merchant.

VOLPONE. [*Lies down as before.*]   Dead.

MOSCA. Another bout, sir, with your eyes. [*Anointing them.*]
   Who's there?

Act I, Scene v

[*Enter to them*] CORVINO.

[MOSCA.] Signor Corvino! come most wished for! O,
   How happy were you, if you knew it, now!

CORVINO. Why? What? Wherein?

MOSCA.   The tardy hour is come, sir.

CORVINO. He is not dead?

MOSCA.   Not dead, sir, but as good;
    He knows no man.

CORVINO.   How shall I do then?

MOSCA.   Why, sir?   5

CORVINO. I have brought him here a pearl.

MOSCA.   Perhaps he has
    So much remembrance left as to know you, sir.
    He still calls on you; nothing but your name
    Is in his mouth. Is your pearl orient, sir?

CORVINO. Venice was never owner of the like.   10

VOLPONE. [*Faintly.*] Signor Corvino.

MOSCA.   Hark.

VOLPONE.   Signor Corvino.

MOSCA. He calls you. Step and give it him. [*To Volpone.*] He's here,
    sir,
    And he has brought you a rich pearl.

CORVINO.   How do you, sir?
    [*To* MOSCA.] Tell him it doubles the twelfth carat.

MOSCA.   Sir,
    He cannot understand, his hearing's gone;   15
    And yet it comforts him to see you –

CORVINO.   Say
    I have a diamond for him, too.

MOSCA.   Best show't, sir;
    Put it into his hand; 'tis only there
    He apprehends. He has his feeling yet.

    [*Volpone seizes the diamond.*]

    See how he grasps it!

CORVINO.   'Las, good gentleman!   20
    How pitiful the sight is!

MOSCA.   Tut, forget, sir.
  The weeping of an heir should still be laughter
  Under a visor.

CORVINO.   Why, am I his heir?

MOSCA. Sir, I am sworn, I may not show the will
  Till he be dead. But here has been Corbaccio,   25
  Here has been Voltore, here were others too,
  I cannot number 'em, they were so many,
  All gaping here for legacies; but I,
  Taking the vantage of his naming you,
  'Signor Corvino, Signor Corvino', took   30
  Paper, and pen, and ink, and there I asked him
  Whom he would have his heir? 'Corvino.' Who
  Should be executor? 'Corvino.' And
  To any question he was silent to,
  I still interpreted the nods he made,   35
  Through weakness, for consent; and sent home th'others,
  Nothing bequeathed them but to cry and curse.

CORVINO. O, my dear Mosca.

They embrace.

                    Does he not perceive us?

MOSCA. No more than a blind harper. He knows no man,
  No face of friend, nor name of any servant,   40
  Who't was that fed him last, or gave him drink;
  Not those he hath begotten, or brought up,
  Can he remember.

CORVINO.   Has he children?

MOSCA.   Bastards,
  Some dozen or more that he begot on beggars,
  Gypsies, and Jews, and black-moors, when he was drunk.   45
  Knew you not that, sir? 'Tis the common fable.
  The dwarf, the fool, the eunuch are all his;
  He's the true father of his family
  In all, save me; but he has given 'em nothing.

CORVINO. That's well, that's well. Art sure he does not hear us? 50

MOSCA. Sure, sir? Why, look you, credit your own sense.

[*Shouts in* VOLPONE*'s ear.*]

The pox approach and add to your diseases,
If it would send you hence the sooner, sir.
For your incontinence, it hath deserved it
Throughly and throughly, and the plague to boot!   55
[*To* CORVINO.] You may come near, sir. [*To* VOLPONE.]
    Would you would once close
Those filthy eyes of yours, that flow with slime
Like two frog-pits, and those same hanging cheeks,
Covered with hide instead of skin – [To CORVINO.] Nay, help,
    sir –
That look like frozen dish-clouts set on end!   60

CORVINO. Or like an old smoked wall, on which the rain
    Ran down in streaks!

MOSCA.   Excellent, sir, speak out.
    You may be louder yet; a culverin
    Discharged in his ear would hardly bore it.

CORVINO. His nose is like a common sewer, still running.   65

MOSCA. 'Tis good! And what his mouth?

CORVINO.   A very draught.

MOSCA. [*Snatching up a pillow.*] O, stop it up –

CORVINO.   By no means.

MOSCA.   Pray you, let me.
    Faith, I could stifle him rarely with a pillow
    As well as any woman that should keep him.

CORVINO. Do as you will, but I'll be gone.

MOSCA.   Be so.   70
    It is your presence makes him last so long.

CORVINO. I pray you, use no violence.

MOSCA.   No, sir? Why?
  Why should you be thus scrupulous, pray you, sir?

CORVINO. Nay, at your discretion.

MOSCA.   Well, good sir, begone.

CORVINO. I will not trouble him now to take my pearl?   75

MOSCA. Pooh! nor your diamond! What a needless care
  Is this afflicts you? [*Takes the pearl*.] Is not all here yours?
  Am not I here? whom you have made? your creature?
  That owe my being to you?

CORVINO.   Grateful Mosca!
  Thou art my friend, my fellow, my companion,   80
  My partner, and shalt share in all my fortunes.

MOSCA. Excepting one.

CORVINO.   What's that?

MOSCA.   Your gallant wife, sir.

  [*Exit* CORVINO.]

  [*To* VOLPONE.] Now he is gone; we had no other means
  To shoot him hence but this.

VOLPONE.   My divine Mosca!
  Thou hast today outgone thyself.

  Another knocks.

                         Who's there?   85
  I will be troubled with no more. Prepare
  Me music, dances, banquets, all delights;
  The Turk is not more sensual in his pleasures
  Than will Volpone.

  [*Exit* MOSCA.]

              Let me see: a pearl!
  A diamond! plate! *chequins*! – good morning's purchase.   90
  Why, this is better than rob churches yet,
  Or fat by eating, once a month, a man.

[*Enter* MOSCA.]

Who is't?

MOSCA.   The beauteous Lady Would-be, sir,
    Wife to the English knight, Sir Politic Would-be –
    This is the style, sir, is directed me –   95
    Hath sent to know how you have slept tonight,
    And if you would be visited?

VOLPONE.   Not now.
    Some three hours hence –

MOSCA.   I told the squire so much.

VOLPONE. When I am high with mirth and wine, then, then.
    'Fore heaven, I wonder at the desperate valour   100
    Of the bold English, that they dare let loose
    Their wives to all encounters!

MOSCA.   Sir, this knight
    Had not his name for nothing: he is politic,
    And knows, howe'er his wife affect strange airs,
    She hath not yet the face to be dishonest.   105
    But had she Signor Corvino's wife's face –

VOLPONE. Hath she so rare a face?

MOSCA.   O, sir, the wonder,
    The blazing star of Italy! a wench
    O' the first year! a beauty, ripe as harvest!
    Whose skin is whiter than a swan, all over!   110
    Than silver, snow, or lilies! a soft lip,
    Would tempt you to eternity of kissing!
    And flesh that melteth in the touch to blood!
    Bright as your gold! and lovely as your gold!

VOLPONE. Why had not I known this before?

MOSCA.   Alas, sir,   115
    Myself but yesterday discovered it.

VOLPONE. How might I see her?

MOSCA.   O, not possible;
    She's kept as warily as is your gold,
    Never does come abroad, never takes air
    But at a window. All her looks are sweet   120
    As the first grapes or cherries, and are watched
    As near as they are.

VOLPONE.   I must see her –

MOSCA.   Sir,
    There is a guard of ten spies thick upon her;
    All his whole household; each of which is set
    Upon his fellow, and have all their charge,   125
    When he goes out, when he comes in, examined.

VOLPONE. I will go see her, though but at her window.

MOSCA. In some disguise then.

VOLPONE.   That is true. I must
    Maintain mine own shape still the same: we'll think.

    [*Exeunt.*]

Act II, Scene i

[*Enter* SIR] POLITIC WOULD-BE [*and*] PEREGRINE.

[SIR POLITIC.] Sir, to a wise man all the world's his soil.
    It is not Italy, nor France, nor Europe
    That must bound me, if my fates call me forth.
    Yet, I protest, it is no salt desire
    Of seeing countries, shifting a religion,   5
    Nor any disaffection to the state
    Where I was bred, and unto which I owe
    My dearest plots, hath brought me out; much less
    That idle, antique, stale, grey-haired project
    Of knowing men's minds and manners, with Ulysses;   10
    But a peculiar humour of my wife's,
    Laid for this height of Venice, to observe,
    To quote, to learn the language, and so forth –
    I hope you travel, sir, with licence?

PEREGRINE.   Yes.

SIR POLITIC. I dare the safelier converse – How long, sir,   15
    Since you left England?

PEREGRINE.   Seven weeks.

SIR POLITIC.   So lately!
    You ha' not been with my lord ambassador?

PEREGRINE. Not yet, sir.

SIR POLITIC.   Pray you, what news, sir, vents our climate?
    I heard, last night, a most strange thing reported
    By some of my lord's followers, and I long   20
    To hear how 'twill be seconded.

PEREGRINE.   What was't, sir?

SIR POLITIC. Marry, sir, of a raven that should build
   In a ship royal of the king's.

PEREGRINE. [*Aside.*]   This fellow,
   Does he gull me, trow? or is gulled? [*To* SIR POLITIC.]
   Your name, sir?

SIR POLITIC.   My name is Politic Would-be.

PEREGRINE. [*Aside.*] O, that speaks him.   25
   [*To* SIR POLITIC.] A knight, sir?

SIR POLITIC.   A poor knight, sir.

PEREGRINE.   Your lady
   Lies here in Venice for intelligence
   Of tires, and fashions, and behaviour
   Among the courtesans? the fine Lady Would-be?

SIR POLITIC. Yes, sir; the spider and the bee oft times   30
   Suck from one flower.

PEREGRINE.   Good Sir Politic,
   I cry you mercy! I have heard much of you.
   'Tis true, sir, of your raven.

SIR POLITIC.   On your knowledge?

PEREGRINE. Yes, and your lion's whelping in the Tower.

SIR POLITIC. Another whelp!

PEREGRINE.   Another, sir.

SIR POLITIC.   Now heaven!   35
   What prodigies be these? The fires at Berwick!
   And the new star! These things concurring, strange!
   And full of omen! Saw you those meteors?

PEREGRINE. I did, sir.

SIR POLITIC.   Fearful! Pray you, sir, confirm me,
   Were there three porpoises seen above the Bridge,   40
   As they give out?

PEREGRINE.   Six, and a sturgeon, sir.

SIR POLITIC. I am astonished!

PEREGRINE.   Nay, sir, be not so;
   I'll tell you a greater prodigy than these –

SIR POLITIC. What should these things portend!

PEREGRINE.   The very day
   (Let me be sure) that I put forth from London,   45
   There was a whale discovered in the river
   As high as Woolwich, that had waited there, .
   Few know how many months, for the subversion
   Of the Stode fleet.

SIR POLITIC.   Is't possible? Believe it,
   'Twas either sent from Spain, or the Archdukes –   50
   Spinola's whale, upon my life, my credit!
   Will they not leave these projects? Worthy sir,
   Some other news.

PEREGRINE.   Faith, Stone the fool is dead,
   And they do lack a tavern fool extremely.

SIR POLITIC. Is Mas' Stone dead?

PEREGRINE.   He's dead, sir; why? I hope   55
   You thought him not immortal? [*Aside.*] O, this knight,
   Were he well known, would be a precious thing
   To fit our English stage: he that should write
   But such a fellow, should be thought to feign
   Extremely, if not maliciously.

SIR POLITIC.   Stone dead!   60

PEREGRINE. Dead. Lord! how deeply, sir, you apprehend it!
   He was no kinsman to you?

SIR POLITIC.   That I know of.
   Well, that same fellow was an unknown fool.

PEREGRINE. And yet you knew him, it seems?

SIR POLITIC.   I did so. Sir,
   I knew him one of the most dangerous heads   65

Living within the state, and so I held him.

PEREGRINE. Indeed, sir?

SIR POLITIC.   While he lived, in action.
   He has received weekly intelligence,
   Upon my knowledge, out of the Low Countries,
   For all parts of the world, in cabbages;   70
   And those dispersed again t'ambassadors
   In oranges, musk-melons, apricots,
   Lemons, pome-citrons, and suchlike; sometimes
   In Colchester oysters, and your Selsey cockles.

PEREGRINE. You make me wonder!

SIR POLITIC.   Sir, upon my knowledge. 75
   Nay, I've observed him at your public ordinary
   Take his advertisement from a traveller
   (A concealed statesman) in a trencher of meat;
   And instantly, before the meal was done,
   Convey an answer in a toothpick.

PEREGRINE.   Strange!   80
   How could this be, sir?

SIR POLITIC.   Why, the meat was cut
   So like his character, and so laid, as he
   Must easily read the cypher.

PEREGRINE.   I have heard
   He could not read, sir.

SIR POLITIC.   So 'twas given out,
   In polity, by those that did employ him;   85
   But he could read, and had your languages,
   And to't as sound a noddle –

PEREGRINE.   I have heard, sir,
   That your *babiouns* were spies, and that they were
   A kind of subtle nation near to China.

SIR POLITIC. Ay, ay, your *Mamaluchi*. Faith, they had 90
   Their hand in a French plot or two; but they

Were so extremely given to women, as
They made discovery of all; yet I
Had my advices here, on Wednesday last,
From one of their own coat, they were returned,   95
Made their relations, as the fashion is,
And now stand fair for fresh employment.

PEREGRINE. [*Aside.*]   'Heart!
     This Sir Pol will be ignorant of nothing.
     [*To* SIR POLITIC.] It seems, sir, you know all.

SIR POLITIC.   Not all, sir. But
     I have some general notions. I do love   100
     To note and to observe; though I live out,
     Free from the active torrent, yet I'd mark
     The currents and the passages of things
     For mine own private use, and know the ebbs
     And flows of state.

PEREGRINE.   Believe it, sir, I hold   105
     Myself in no small tie unto my fortunes
     For casting me thus luckily upon you,
     Whose knowledge, if your bounty equal it,
     May do me great assistance in instruction
     For my behaviour, and my bearing, which   110
     Is yet so rude and raw –

SIR POLITIC.   Why, came you forth
     Empty of rules for travel?

PEREGRINE.   Faith, I had
     Some common ones from out that vulgar grammar
     Which he that cried Italian to me taught me.

SIR POLITIC. Why, this it is that spoils all our brave bloods,   115
     Trusting our hopeful gentry unto pedants,
     Fellows of outside and mere bark. You seem
     To be a gentleman of ingenuous race –
     I not profess it, but my fate hath been
     To be where I have been consulted with,   120
     In this high kind, touching some great men's sons,

Persons of blood and honour –

PEREGRINE.   Who be these, sir?

Act II, Scene ii

[*Enter to them*] MOSCA [*and*] NANO [*disguised as zanies and followed by*] GREGE [*, the crowd*].

[MOSCA.] Under that window, there't must be. The same.

   [MOSCA *and* NANO *set up a rostrum.*]

SIR POLITIC. Fellows to mount a bank! Did your instructor
   In the dear tongues never discourse to you
   Of the Italian mountebanks?

PEREGRINE.   Yes, sir.

SIR POLITIC.   Why,
   Here shall you see one.

PEREGRINE.   They are quacksalvers,   5
   Fellows that live by venting oils and drugs?

SIR POLITIC. Was that the character he gave you of them?

PEREGRINE. As I remember.

SIR POLITIC.   Pity his ignorance.
   They are the only knowing men of Europe!
   Great general scholars, excellent physicians,   10
   Most admired statesmen, professed favourites
   And cabinet counsellors to the greatest princes!
   The only languaged men of all the world!

PEREGRINE. And I have heard they are most lewd impostors,
   Made all of terms and shreds; no less beliers   15
   Of great men's favours than their own vile med'cines;
   Which they will utter upon monstrous oaths,
   Selling that drug for twopence, ere they part,
   Which they have valued at twelve crowns before.

SIR POLITIC. Sir, calumnies are answered best with silence.   20
    Yourself shall judge. [*To* MOSCA *and* NANO.] Who is it mounts,
      my friends?

MOSCA. Scoto of Mantua, sir.

SIR POLITIC.   Is't he? Nay, then
    I'll proudly promise, sir, you shall behold
    Another man than has been phant'sied to you.
    I wonder, yet, that he should mount his bank   25
    Here, in this nook, that has been wont t'appear
    In face of the Piazza! Here he comes.

    [*Enter* VOLPONE, *disguised as a mountebank.*]

VOLPONE. [*To* NANO.] Mount, zany.

GREGE.   Follow, follow, follow, follow, follow.

SIR POLITIC. See how the people follow him! He's a man
    May write ten thousand crowns in bank here. Note;   30

    [VOLPONE *mounts the rostrum.*]

    Mark but his gesture. I do use to observe
    The state he keeps in getting up!

PEREGRINE.   'Tis worth it, sir.

VOLPONE. Most noble gentlemen, and my worthy patrons, it
    may seem strange that I, your Scoto Mantuano, who was
    ever wont to fix my bank in face of the public Piazza,   35
    near the shelter of the portico to the Procuratia, should
    now after eight months' absence from this illustrious city
    of Venice, humbly retire myself into an obscure nook of
    the Piazza.

SIR POLITIC. Did not I now object the same?

PEREGRINE.   Peace, sir.   40

VOLPONE. Let me tell you: I am not, as your Lombard
    proverb saith, cold on my feet, or content to part with
    my commodities at a cheaper rate than I accustomed.
    Look not for it. Nor that the calumnious reports of that

impudent detractor and shame to our profession   45
(Alessandro Buttone, I mean), who gave out in public
I was condemned a *sforzato* to the galleys for poisoning
the Cardinal Bembo's – cook, hath at all attached, much
less dejected me. No, no, worthy gentlemen; to tell you
true, I cannot endure to see the rabble of these ground   50
ciarlitani that spread their cloaks on the pavement as if
they meant to do feats of activity, and then come in
lamely with their mouldy tales out of Boccaccio, like stale
Tabarin, the fabulist: some of them discoursing their
travels, and of their tedious captivity in the Turks'   55
galleys, when, indeed, were the truth known, they were
the Christians' galleys, where very temperately they ate
bread and drunk water, as a wholesome penance
enjoined them by their confessors for base pilferies.

SIR POLITIC. Note but his bearing and contempt of these.   60

VOLPONE. These turdy-facy-nasty-paty-lousy-fartical rogues,
with one poor groatsworth of unprepared antimony,
finely wrapped up in several *scartoccios*, are able very well
to kill their twenty a week, and play; yet these meagre,
starved spirits, who have half stopped the organs of their 65
minds with earthy oppilations, want not their favourers
among your shrivelled salad-eating artizans, who are
overjoyed that they may have their ha'p'orth of physic;
though it purge 'em into another world, 't makes no
matter.   70

SIR POLITIC. Excellent! Ha' you heard better language, sir?

VOLPONE. Well, let 'em go. And, gentlemen, honourable
gentlemen, know that for this time our bank, being thus
removed from the clamours of the *canaglia*, shall be the
scene of pleasure and delight; for I have nothing to sell, 75
little or nothing to sell.

SIR POLITIC. I told you, sir, his end.

PEREGRINE.   You did so, sir.

VOLPONE. I protest, I and my six servants are not able to make

of this precious liquor so fast as it is fetched away from my
lodging by gentlemen of your city, strangers of the *Terra*   80
Firma, worshipful merchants, ay, and senators too, who,
ever since my arrival, have detained me to their uses by
their splendidous liberalities. And worthily! For what
avails your rich man to have his magazines stuffed with
moscadelli, or of the purest grape, when his physicians   85
prescribe him, on pain of death, to drink nothing but
water cocted with aniseeds? O, health! health! the
blessing of the rich! the riches of the poor! who can
buy thee at too dear a rate, since there is no enjoying
this world without thee? Be not then so sparing of your   90
purses, honourable gentlemen, as to abridge the natural
course of life –

PEREGRINE. You see his end?

SIR POLITIC.   Ay, is't not good?

VOLPONE. For when a humid flux, or catarrh, by the mutability
of air, falls from your head into an arm or shoulder, or any   95
other part, take you a *ducat*, or your *chequin* of gold, and
apply to the place affected: see what good effect it can
work. No, no, 'tis this blessed *unguento*, this rare extrac-
tion, that hath only power to disperse all malignant
humours that proceed either of hot, cold, moist, or windy
causes –   100

PEREGRINE. I would he had put in dry too.

SIR POLITIC.   Pray you, observe.

VOLPONE. To fortify the most indigest and crude stomach;
ay, were it of one that through extreme weakness vomited
blood, applying only a warm napkin to the place, after   105
the unction and the fricace; for the *vertiginè* in the head,
putting but a drop unto your nostrils, likewise behind
the ears – a most sovereign and approved remedy; the
mal caduco, cramps, convulsions, paralyses, epilepsies,
tremor cordia, retired nerves, ill vapours of the spleen,   110
stoppings of the liver, the stone, the strangury, *hernia*

ventosa, iliaca passio; stops a *dysenteria* immediately;
easeth the torsion of the small guts; and cures *melan-*
cholia hypocondriaca, being taken and applied according
to my printed receipt.   115

Pointing to his bill and his glass.

For this is the physician, this the medicine; this counsels,
this cures; this gives the direction, this works the effect;
and, in sum, both together may be termed an abstract of
the theoric and practic in the Aesculapian art. 'Twill
cost you eight crowns. [*To* NANO.] And, Zan Fritada,   120
pray thee sing a verse *extempore* in honour of it.

SIR POLITIC. How do you like him, sir?

PEREGRINE.   Most strangely, I!

SIR POLITIC. Is not his language rare?

PEREGRINE.   But alchemy
I never heard the like, or Broughton's books.

Song.

[NANO.] Had old Hippocrates, or Galen,   125
That to their books put med'cines all in,
But known this secret, they had never
(Of which they will be guilty ever)
Been murderers of so much paper,
Or wasted many a hurtless taper;   130
No Indian drug had e'er been famed,
Tobacco, sassafras not named;
Ne yet of guacum one small stick, sir,
Nor Raymond Lully's great elixir;
Nor had been known the Danish Gonswart,   135
Or Paracelsus with his long sword.

PEREGRINE. All this, yet, will not do. Eight crowns is high.

VOLPONE. No more. Gentlemen, if I had but time to discourse
to you the miraculous effects of this my oil, surnamed
Oglio del Scoto, with the countless catalogue of those I   140

have cured of the aforesaid, and many more diseases; the
patents and privileges of all the princes and common-
wealths of Christendom; or but the depositions of those
that appeared on my part before the Signiory of the
Sanita and most learned College of Physicians, where   145
I was authorised, upon notice taken of the admirable
virtues of my medicaments and mine own excellency in
matter of rare and unknown secrets, not only to disperse
them publicly in this famous city, but in all the territories
that happily joy under the government of the most pious   150
and magnificent states of Italy. But may some other
gallant say, 'O, there be divers that make profession to
have as good and as experimented receipts as yours!'
Indeed, very many have assayed, like apes, in imitation
of that which is really and essentially in me, to make of   155
this oil; bestowed great cost in furnaces, stills, alembics,
continual fires, and preparation of the ingredients (as
indeed there goes to it six hundred several simples,
besides some quantity of human fat, for the congluti-
nation, which we buy of anatomists); but, when these   160
practitioners come to the last decoction, blow, blow,
puff, puff – and all flies in *fumo*: ha, ha, ha! Poor
wretches! I rather pity their folly and indiscretion than
their loss of time and money; for those may be recovered
by industry, but to be a fool born is a disease incurable.   165
For myself, I always from my youth have endeavoured
to get the rarest secrets, and book them, either in
exchange or for money; I spared nor cost nor labour
where anything was worthy to be learned. And gentlemen, honourable gentlemen, I will undertake, by virtue   170
of chemical art, out of the honourable hat that covers your
head to extract the four elements, that is to say, the fire,
air, water, and earth, and return you your felt without
burn or stain. For, whilst others have been at the *balloo*,
I have been at my book, and am now past the craggy   175
paths of study, and come to the flowery plains of honour
and reputation.

SIR POLITIC. I do assure, you sir, that is his aim.

VOLPONE. But to our price.

PEREGRINE.   And that withal, Sir Pol.

VOLPONE. You all know, honourable gentlemen, I never   180
    valued this *ampulla*, or vial, at less than eight crowns; but
    for this time I am content to be deprived of it for six: six
    crowns is the price, and less, in courtesy, I know you
    cannot offer me. Take it or leave it, howsoever, both it
    and I am at your service. I ask you not as the value of   185
    the thing, for then I should demand of you a thousand
    crowns: so the Cardinals Montalto, Fernese, the great
    Duke of Tuscany, my gossip, with divers other princes,
    have given me; but I despise money. Only to show my
    affection to you, honourable gentlemen, and your   190
    illustrous state here, I have neglected the messages of
    these princes, mine own offices, framed my journey
    hither, only to present you with the fruits of my travels.
    [*To* NANO *and* MOSCA.] Tune your voices once more
    to the touch of your instruments, and give the honourable   195
    assembly some delightful recreation.

PEREGRINE. What monstrous and most painful circumstance
    Is here, to get some three or four *gazets*,
    Some threepence i' th' whole – for that 'twill come to!

    [*During the*] song [, CELIA *appears at a window above*].

[NANO.] You that would last long, list to my song,   200
    Make no more coil, but buy of this oil.
    Would you be ever fair? and young?
    Stout of teeth? and strong of tongue?
    Tart of palate? quick of ear?
    Sharp of sight? of nostril clear?   205
    Moist of hand? and light of foot?
    Or I will come nearer to 't,
    Would you live free from all diseases?
    Do the act your mistress pleases,
    Yet fright all aches from your bones?   210

Here's a med'cine for the nones.

VOLPONE. Well, I am in a humour, at this time, to make
a present of the small quantity my coffer contains, to the
rich in courtesy, and to the poor for God's sake. Wherefore, now mark: I asked you six crowns, and six crowns   215
at other times you have paid me. You shall not give me
six crowns, nor five, nor four, nor three, nor two, nor
one; nor half a *ducat*; no, nor a *moccenigo*. Six – pence it
will cost you, or six-hundred pound – expect no lower
price, for, by the banner of my front, I will not bate a   220
bagatine: that I will have, only, a pledge of your loves,
to carry something from amongst you to show I am not
contemned by you. Therefore, now toss your hand-
kerchiefs cheerfully, cheerfully; and be advertised that
the first heroic spirit that deigns to grace me with a   225
handkerchief, I will give it a little remembrance of
something beside, shall please it better than if I had
presented it with a double *pistolet*.

PEREGRINE. Will you be that heroic spark, Sir Pol?

CELIA *at the window throws down her handkerchief.*

O, see! the window has prevented you.   230

VOLPONE. Lady, I kiss your bounty; and for this timely grace
you have done your poor Scoto of Mantua, I will return
you, over and above my oil, a secret of that high and
inestimable nature shall make you for ever enamoured
on that minute wherein your eye first descended on so   235
mean (yet not altogether to be despised) an object. Here
is a powder concealed in this paper of which, if I should
speak to the worth, nine thousand volumes were but as
one page, that page as a line, that line as a word; so short
is this pilgrimage of man (which some call life) to the   240
expressing of it. Would I reflect on the price, why, the
whole world were but as an empire, that empire as a
province, that province as a bank, that bank as a private
purse, to the purchase of it. I will only tell you: it is the
powder that made Venus a goddess, given her by Apollo,   245

that kept her perpetually young, cleared her wrinkles,
firmed her gums, filled her skin, coloured her hair. From
her derived to Helen, and at the sack of Troy – unfortu-
nately – lost; till now, in this our age, it was as happily
recovered by a studious antiquary, out of some ruins of   250
Asia, who sent a moiety of it to the court of France (but
much sophisticated), wherewith the ladies there now
colour their hair. The rest, at this present, remains with
me; extracted to a quintessence, so that, wherever it but
touches, in youth it perpetually preserves, in age restores   255
the complexion; seats your teeth, did they dance like virginal
jacks, firm as a wall; makes them white as ivory, that were
black as –

Act II, Scene iii

[*Enter to them*] CORVINO.

[CORVINO.] [*To* CELIA.] Blood of the devil, and my shame!
   [*To* VOLPONE.] Come down here, Come down!
   No house but mine to make your scene?
   Signor Flamineo, will you down, sir? down!
   What, is my wife your *Franciscina*, sir?
   No windows on the whole Piazza here   5
   To make your properties but mine? – but mine?

   He beats away the mountebank, etc. [*and* CELIA *leaves the window.*]

   Heart! ere tomorrow I shall be new christened
   And called the *Pantalone di Besogniosi*,
   About the town.

   [*Exit* CORVINO; *the* CROWD *disperses.*]

PEREGRINE.   What should this mean, Sir Pol?

SIR POLITIC. Some trick of state, believe it. I will home.   10

PEREGRINE. It may be some design on you.

SIR POLITIC.   I know not.

I'll stand upon my guard.

PEREGRINE.   It is your best, sir.

SIR POLITIC. This three weeks all my advices, all my letters,
    They have been intercepted.

PEREGRINE.   Indeed, sir?
    Best have a care.

SIR POLITIC.   Nay, so I will. [*Exit.*]

PEREGRINE.   This knight,   15
    I may not lose him for my mirth, till night. [*Exit.*]

Act II, Scene iv

[*Enter*] VOLPONE [*and*] MOSCA.

[VOLPONE.] O, I am wounded!

MOSCA.   Where, sir?

VOLPONE.   Not without;
    Those blows were nothing, I could bear them ever.
    But angry Cupid, bolting from her eyes,
    Hath shot himself into me like a flame;
    Where now he flings about his burning heat,   5
    As in a furnace an ambitious fire
    Whose vent is stopped. The fight is all within me.
    I cannot live except thou help me, Mosca;
    My liver melts, and I, without the hope
    Of some soft air from her refreshing breath,   10
    Am but a heap of cinders.

MOSCA.   'Las, good sir!
    Would you had never seen her.

VOLPONE.   Nay, would thou
    Hadst never told me of her.

MOSCA.   Sir, 'tis true;

I do confess I was unfortunate
And you unhappy; but I'm bound in conscience,   15
No less than duty, to effect my best
To your release of torment, and I will, sir,

VOLPONE. Dear Mosca, shall I hope?

MOSCA.   Sir, more than dear,
I will not bid you to despair of aught
Within a human compass.

VOLPONE.   O, there spoke   20
My better angel. Mosca, take my keys:
Gold, plate, and jewels, all's at thy devotion;
Employ them how thou wilt. Nay, coin me too,
So thou in this but crown my longings. – Mosca?

MOSCA. Use but your patience.

VOLPONE.   So I have.

MOSCA.   I doubt not   25
To bring success to your desires.

VOLPONE.   Nay, then,
I not repent me of my late disguise.

MOSCA. If you can horn him, sir, you need not.

VOLPONE.   True.
Besides, I never meant him for my heir.
Is not the colour o' my beard and eyebrows   30
To make me known?

MOSCA.   No jot.

VOLPONE.   I did it well.

MOSCA. So well, would I could follow you in mine,
With half the happiness! And yet, I would
Escape your epilogue.

VOLPONE.   But were they gulled
With a belief that I was Scoto?

MOSCA.   Sir,   35

Scoto himself could hardly have distinguished!
I have not time to flatter you now; we'll part,
And as I prosper, so applaud my art. [*Exeunt.*]

Act II, Scene v

[*Enter*] CORVINO [*and*] CELIA.

[CORVINO.] Death of mine honour, with the city's fool?
   A juggling, tooth-drawing, prating mountebank?
   And at a public window? where, whilst he
   With his strained action and his dole of faces
   To his drug-lecture draws your itching ears,   5
   A crew of old, unmarried, noted lechers
   Stood leering up like satyrs? And you smile
   Most graciously! and fan your favours forth,
   To give your hot spectators satisfaction!
   What, was your mountebank their call? their whistle?   10
   Or were you enamoured on his copper rings?
   His saffron jewel with the toad-stone in't?
   Or his embroidered suit with the cope-stitch,
   Made of a hearse cloth? or his old tilt-feather?
   Or his starched beard? Well, you shall have him, yes!   15
   He shall come home and minister unto you
   The fricace for the mother. Or, let me see,
   I think you'd rather mount? would you not mount?
   Why, if you'll mount, you may; yes truly, you may –
   And so you may be seen down to th' foot.   20
   Get you a cittern, Lady Vanity,
   And be a dealer with the Virtuous Man;
   Make one. I'll but protest myself a cuckold,
   And save your dowry. I am a Dutchman, I!
   For if you thought me an Italian,   25
   You would be damned ere you did this, you whore;
   Thou'dst tremble to imagine that the murder
   Of father, mother, brother, all thy race,
   Should follow as the subject of my justice!

CELIA. Good sir, have patience!

CORVINO. [*Drawing a dagger.*]   What couldst thou propose   30
  Less to thyself than, in this heat of wrath
  And stung with my dishonour, I should strike
  This steel into thee, with as many stabs
  As thou wert gazed upon with goatish eyes?

CELIA. Alas, sir, be appeased! I could not think   35
  My being at the window should more now
  Move your impatience than at other times.

CORVINO. No? Not to seek and entertain a parley
  With a known knave? before a multitude?
  You were an actor, with your handkerchief!   40
  Which he most sweetly kissed in the receipt,
  And might, no doubt, return it with a letter,
  And point the place where you might meet – your sister's,
  Your mother's, or your aunt's might serve the turn.

CELIA. Why, dear sir, when do I make these excuses?   45
  Or ever stir abroad but to the church?
  And that so seldom –

CORVINO.   Well, it shall be less;
  And thy restraint before was liberty
  To what I now decree. And therefore mark me.
  First, I will have this bawdy light dammed up;   50
  And, till't be done, some two or three yards off
  I'll chalk a line, o'er which if thou but chance
  To set thy desp'rate foot, more hell, more horror,
  More wild, remorseless rage shall seize on thee
  Than on a conjuror that had heedless left   55
  His circle's safety ere his devil was laid.

[*Showing her a chastity belt.*]

  Then, here's a lock which I will hang upon thee;
  And, now I think on't, I will keep thee backwards:
  Thy lodging shall be backwards, thy walks backwards,
  Thy prospect – all be backwards, and no pleasure   60
  That thou shalt know but backwards. Nay, since you force

My honest nature, know it is your own
Being too open makes me use you thus.
Since you will not contain your subtle nostrils
In a sweet room, but they must snuff the air   65
Of rank and sweaty passengers –

Knock within.

                                   One knocks!
Away, and be not seen, pain of thy life;
Not look toward the window; if thou dost –

[CELIA *starts to leave.*]

Nay, stay, hear this: let me not prosper, whore,
But I will make thee an anatomy,   70
Dissect thee mine own self, and read a lecture
Upon thee to the city, and in public.
Away! [*Exit* CELIA.]
                    Who's there? [*Enter* SERVANT.]

SERVANT.   'Tis Signor Mosca, sir.

Act II, Scene vi

[CORVINO.] Let him come in. [*Exit* SERVANT.]
                              His master's dead! There's yet
    Some good to help the bad. [*Enter to him* MOSCA.]
                                        My Mosca, welcome!
    I guess your news.

MOSCA.   I fear you cannot, sir.

CORVINO. Is't not his death?

MOSCA.   Rather the contrary.

CORVINO. Not his recovery?

MOSCA.   Yes, sir.

CORVINO.   I am cursed,   5

I am bewitched; my crosses meet to vex me.
How? how? how? how?

MOSCA.   Why, sir, with Scoto's oil!
  Corbaccio and Voltore brought of it,
  While I was busy in an inner room –

CORVINO. Death! that damned mountebank! But for the law,   10
  Now I could kill the rascal; 't cannot be
  His oil should have that virtue. Ha' not I
  Known him a common rogue, come fiddling in
  To th'*osteria*, with a tumbling whore,
  And, when he has done all his forced tricks, been glad   15
  Of a poor spoonful of dead wine, with flies in't?
  It cannot be. All his ingredients
  Are a sheep's gall, a roasted bitch's marrow,
  Some few sod earwigs, pounded caterpillars,
  A little capon's grease, and fasting spittle;   20
  I know 'em to a dram.

MOSCA.   I know not, sir;
  But some on't, there, they poured into his ears,
  Some in his nostrils, and recovered him,
  Applying but the fricace.

CORVINO.   Pox o' that fricace!

MOSCA. And since, to seem the more officious   25
  And flatt'ring of his health, there they have had,
  At extreme fees, the college of physicians
  Consulting on him how they might restore him;
  Where one would have a cataplasm of spices,
  Another a flayed ape clapped to his breast,   30
  A third would ha' it a dog, a fourth an oil
  With wildcats' skins. At last they all resolved
  That to preserve him was no other means
  But some young woman must be straight sought out,
  Lusty, and full of juice, to sleep by him;   35
  And to this service, most unhappily
  And most unwillingly, am I now employed,
  Which here I thought to pre-acquaint you with,

For your advice, since it concerns you most;
Because I would not do that thing might cross   40
Your ends, on whom I have my whole dependence, sir.
Yet, if I do it not, they may delate
My slackness to my patron, work me out
Of his opinion; and there all your hopes,
Ventures, or whatsoever, are all frustrate.   45
I do but tell you, sir. Besides, they are all
Now striving who shall first present him. Therefore –
I could entreat you, briefly, conclude somewhat.
Prevent 'em if you can.

CORVINO.   Death to my hopes!
This is my villainous fortune! Best to hire   50
Some common courtesan?

MOSCA.   Ay, I thought on that, sir.
But they are all so subtle, full of art,
And age again doting and flexible,
So as – I cannot tell – we may perchance
Light on a quean may cheat us all.

CORVINO.   'Tis true.   55

MOSCA. No, no; it must be one that has no tricks, sir,
Some simple thing, a creature made unto it;
Some wench you may command. Ha' you no kinswoman?
Godso – Think, think, think, think, think, think, think, sir.
One o' the doctors offered there his daughter.   60

CORVINO. How!

MOSCA.   Yes, Signor Lupo, the physician.

CORVINO. His daughter?

MOSCA.   And a virgin sir. Why, alas,
He knows the state of's body, what it is:
That nought can warm his blood, sir, but a fever;
Nor any incantation raise his spirit;   65
A long forgetfulness hath seized that part.
Besides, sir, who shall know it? Some one or two –

CORVINO. I pray thee give me leave.

[*Walks aside, pondering.*]

                                If any man
But I had had this luck – The thing in'tself
I know is nothing – Wherefore should not I   70
As well command my blood and my affections
As this dull doctor? In the point of honour,
The cases are all one of wife and daughter.

MOSCA. [*Aside.*] I hear him coming.

CORVINO. [*Aside.*]   She shall do't. 'Tis done.
'Slight, if this doctor, who is not engaged,   75
Unless't be for his counsel (which is nothing),
Offer his daughter, what should I that am
So deeply in? I will prevent him; wretch!
Covetous wretch! [*To* MOSCA.] Mosca, I have determined.

MOSCA. How, sir?

CORVINO.   We'll make all sure. The party you wot of   80
Shall be mine own wife, Mosca.

MOSCA.   Sir, the thing –
But that I would not seem to counsel you –
I should have motioned to you at the first.
And, make your count, you have cut all their throats.
Why, 'tis directly taking a possession!   85
And in his next fit, we may let him go.
'Tis but to pull the pillow from his head,
And he is throttled; 't had been done before
But for your scrupulous doubts.

CORVINO.   Ay, a plague on't;
My conscience fools my wit! Well, I'll be brief,   90
And so be thou, lest they should be before us.
Go home, prepare him, tell him with what zeal
And willingness I do it; swear it was
On the first hearing, as thou mayst do truly,
Mine own free motion.

MOSCA.   Sir, I warrant you   95
  I'll so possess him with it, that the rest
  Of his starved clients shall be banished all,
  And only you received. But come not, sir,
  Until I send, for I have something else
  To ripen for your good; you must not know't.   100

CORVINO. But do not you forget to send now.

MOSCA.   Fear not. [*Exit.*]

Act II, Scene vii

[CORVINO.] Where are you, wife? My Celia? wife!

  [*Enter to him* CELIA, *crying.*]
                                  What, blubbering?
  Come, dry those tears. I think thou thought'st me in earnest?
  Ha? By this light I talked so but to try thee.
  Methinks the lightness of the occasion
  Should ha' confirmed thee. Come, I am not jealous.   5

CELIA. No?

CORVINO. Faith, I am not, I, nor never was;
  It is a poor, unprofitable humour.
  Do not I know if women have a will
  They'll do 'gainst all the watches o' the world?
  And that the fiercest spies are tamed with gold?   10
  Tut, I'm confident in thee, thou shalt see't;
  And see, I'll give thee cause too, to believe it.
  Come, kiss me. [CELIA *kisses him.*] Go, and make thee ready
    straight
  In all thy best attire, thy choicest jewels,
  Put 'em all on, and with 'em thy best looks.   15
  We are invited to a solemn feast
  At old Volpone's, where it shall appear
  How far I'm free from jealousy or fear. [*Exeunt.*]

Act III, Scene i

[*Enter*] MOSCA.

[MOSCA.] I fear I shall begin to grow in love
    With my dear self and my most prosp'rous parts,
    They do so spring and burgeon; I can feel
    A whimsy i' my blood. I know not how,
    Success hath made me wanton. I could skip   5
    Out of my skin, now, like a subtle snake,
    I am so limber. O! your parasite
    Is a most precious thing, dropped from above,
    Not bred 'amongst clods and clotpolls here on earth.
    I muse the mystery was not made a science,   10
    It is so liberally professed! Almost
    All the wise world is little else in nature
    But parasites or sub-parasites. And yet
    I mean not those that have your bare town-art,
    To know who's fit to feed 'em; have no house,   15
    No family, no care, and therefore mould
    Tales for men's ears, to bait that sense; or get
    Kitchen-invention, and some stale receipts
    To please the belly, and the groin; nor those,
    With their court-dog-tricks, that can fawn and fleer,   20
    Make their revenue out of legs and faces,
    Echo my lord, and lick away a moth:
    But your fine, elegant rascal, that can rise
    And stoop almost together, like an arrow;
    Shoot through the air as nimbly as a star;   25
    Turn short as doth a swallow; and be here,
    And there, and here, and yonder, all at once;
    Present to any humour, all occasion;
    And change a visor swifter than a thought!
    This is the creature had the art born with him;   30

Toils not to learn it, but doth practise it
Out of most excellent nature: and such sparks
Are the true parasites, others but their zanies.

Act III, Scene ii

[*Enter to him*] BONARIO.

[MOSCA.] [*Aside.*] Who's this? Bonario? Old Corbaccio's son?
    The person I was bound to seek. [*To him.*] Fair sir,
    You are happ'ly met.

BONARIO.   That cannot be by thee.

MOSCA. Why, sir?

BONARIO.   Nay, pray thee know thy way and leave me;
    I would be loath to interchange discourse   5
    With such a mate as thou art.

MOSCA.   Courteous sir,
    Scorn not my poverty.

BONARIO.   Not I, by heaven;
    But thou shalt give me leave to hate thy baseness.

MOSCA. Baseness?

BONARIO.   Ay; answer me, is not thy sloth
    Sufficient argument? thy flattery?   10
    Thy means of feeding?

MOSCA.   Heaven be good to me!
    These imputations are too common, sir,
    And eas'ly stuck on virtue when she's poor.
    You are unequal to me, and howe'er
    Your sentence may be righteous, yet you are not,   15
    That, ere you know me, thus proceed in censure.
    St Mark bear witness 'gainst you, 'tis inhuman. [*Weeps.*]

BONARIO. [*Aside.*] What? does he weep? The sign is soft and good!
    I do repent me that I was so harsh.

MOSCA. 'Tis true that, swayed by strong necessity,   20
    I am enforced to eat my careful bread
    With too much obsequy; 'tis true, beside,
    That I am fain to spin mine own poor raiment
    Out of my mere observance, being not born
    To a free fortune; but that I have done   25
    Base offices in rending friends asunder,
    Dividing families, betraying counsels,
    Whispering false lies, or mining men with praises,
    Trained their credulity with perjuries,
    Corrupted chastity, or am in love   30
    With mine own tender ease, but would not rather
    Prove the most rugged and laborious course
    That might redeem my present estimation,
    Let me here perish in all hope of goodness.

BONARIO. [*Aside.*] This cannot be a personated passion!   35
    [*To him.*] I was to blame, so to mistake thy nature;
    Pray thee forgive me, and speak out thy business.

MOSCA. Sir, it concerns you; and though I may seem
    At first to make a main offence in manners,
    And in my gratitude unto my master,   40
    Yet for the pure love which I bear all right,
    And hatred of the wrong, I must reveal it.
    This very hour your father is in purpose
    To disinherit you –

BONARIO.   How!

MOSCA.   And thrust you forth
    As a mere stranger to his blood: 'tis true, sir,   45
    The work no way engageth me, but as
    I claim an interest in the general state
    Of goodness and true virtue, which I hear
    T'abound in you, and for which mere respect,
    Without a second aim, sir, I have done it.   50

BONARIO. This tale hath lost thee much of the late trust
    Thou hadst with me; it is impossible.
    I know not how to lend it any thought,
    My father should be so unnatural.

MOSCA. It is a confidence that well becomes   55
     Your piety; and formed, no doubt, it is
     From your own simple innocence, which makes
     Your wrong more monstrous and abhorred. But, sir,
     I now will tell you more. This very minute
     It is, or will be, doing; and if you   60
     Shall be but pleased to go with me, I'll bring you –
     I dare not say where you shall see, but – where
     Your ear shall be a witness of the deed;
     Hear yourself written bastard and professed
     The common issue of the earth.

BONARIO.   I'm mazed!   65

MOSCA. Sir, if I do it not, draw your just sword,
     And score your vengeance on my front and face;
     Mark me your villain. You have too much wrong,
     And I do suffer for you, sir. My heart
     Weeps blood in anguish –

BONARIO.   Lead. I follow thee.   70

     [*Exeunt.*]

Act III, Scene iii

[*Enter*] VOLPONE, NANO, ANDROGYNO, [*and*] CASTRONE.

[VOLPONE.] Mosca stays long, methinks. Bring forth your sports
     And help to make the wretched time more sweet.

NANO. Dwarf, fool, and eunuch, well met here we be.
     A question it were now, whether of us three,
     Being, all, the known delicates of a rich man,   5
     In pleasing him claim the precedency can?

CASTRONE. I claim for myself.

ANDROGYNO.   And so doth the fool.

NANO. 'Tis foolish indeed; let me set you both to school.

First for your dwarf: he's little and witty,
    And everything, as it is little, is pretty;   10
Else why do men say to a creature of my shape,
    So soon as they see him, 'It's a pretty little ape'?
And why a pretty 'ape'? but for pleasing imitation
    Of greater men's action, in a ridiculous fashion.
Beside, this feat body of mine doth not crave   15
    Half the meat, drink, and cloth one of your bulks will have.
Admit your fool's face be the mother of laughter,
    Yet, for his brain, it must always come after;
And though that do feed him, it's a pitiful case
    His body is beholding to such a bad face.   20

One knocks.

VOLPONE. Who's there? my couch; away, look Nano, see;
    Give me my caps first – Go, inquire.

[*Exeunt* NANO, CASTRONE, *and* ANDROGYNO.]

[*Volpone gets into bed.*]   Cupid
Send it be Mosca, and with fair return.

[*Re-enter* NANO.]

NANO. It is the beauteous madam –

VOLPONE.   Would-be – is it?

NANO. The same.

VOLPONE.   Now torment on me! Squire her in,   25
    For she will enter, or dwell here forever.
    Nay, quickly, that my fit were past! [*Exit* NANO.] I fear
    A second hell too, that my loathing this
    Will quite expel my appetite to the other.
    Would she were taking now her tedious leave.   30
    Lord, how it threats me, what I am to suffer!

Act III, Scene iv

[*Enter to him*] NANO [*with*] LADY [POLITIC WOULD-BE].

[LADY POLITIC.] [*To* NANO.] I thank you, good sir. Pray you
    signify
Unto your patron I am here. – This band
Shows not my neck enough – I trouble you, sir;
Let me request you bid one of my women
Come hither to me.

[NANO *goes to the door.*]

                 In good faith, I'm dressed   5
Most favourably today! It is no matter:
'Tis well enough.

[*Enter* 1 WOMAN.]

             Look, see, these petulant things,
How they have done this!

VOLPONE. [*Aside.*]   I do feel the fever
Ent'ring in at mine ears. O, for a charm
To fright it hence.

LADY POLITIC. [*To* 1 WOMAN.] Come nearer. Is this curl   10
In his right place? or this? Why is this higher
Than all the rest? You ha' not washed your eyes yet?
Or do they not stand even i' your head?
Where's your fellow? Call her. [*Exit* 1 WOMAN.]

NANO. [*Aside.*]   Now, St. Mark
Deliver us! Anon she'll beat her women   15
Because her nose is red.

[*Re-enter* 1 *with* 2 WOMAN.]

LADY POLITIC.   I pray you, view
This tire, forsooth; are all things apt, or no?

2 WOMAN. One hair a little, here, sticks out, forsooth.

LADY POLITIC. Does't so, forsooth! [*To* 2 WOMAN.] And where
    was your dear sight

When it did so, forsooth? What now! bird-eyed?   20
[*To* 2 WOMAN.] And you too? Pray you both approach and
mend it.
Now, by that light, I muse you're not ashamed!
I, that have preached these things so oft unto you,
Read you the principles, argued all the grounds,
Disputed every fitness, every grace,   25
Called you to counsel of so frequent dressings –

NANO. [*Aside.*] More carefully than of your fame or honour.

LADY POLITIC. Made you acquainted what an ample dowry
The knowledge of these things would be unto you,
Able, alone, to get you noble husbands   30
At your return; and you thus to neglect it!
Besides, you seeing what a curious nation
Th'Italians are, what will they say of me?
'The English lady cannot dress herself.'
Here's a fine imputation to our country!   35
Well, go your ways, and stay i' the next room.
This fucus was too coarse too; it's no matter.
[*To* NANO.] Good sir, you'll give 'em entertainment?

[*Exit* NANO *with* WOMEN.]

VOLPONE. [*Aside.*] The storm comes towards me.

LADY POLITIC. [*Approaches the bed.*]   How does my Volp?

VOLPONE. Troubled with noise, I cannot sleep; I dreamt   40
That a strange fury entered now my house
And with the dreadful tempest of her breath
Did cleave my roof asunder.

LADY POLITIC.   Believe me, and I
Had the most fearful dream, could I remember't –   44

VOLPONE. [*Aside.*] Out on my fate! I ha' giv'n her the occasion
How to torment me: she will tell me hers.

LADY POLITIC. Methought the golden mediocrity,
Polite, and delicate –

VOLPONE.   O, if you do love me,
     No more; I sweat and suffer at the mention
     Of any dream; [*Clutching her.*] feel how I tremble yet.   50

LADY POLITIC. Alas, good soul! the passion of the heart.
     Seed-pearl were good now, boiled with syrup of apples,
     Tincture of gold, and coral, citron-pills,
     Your elecampane root, myrobalanes –   54

VOLPONE. [*Aside.*] Ay me, I have ta'n a grasshopper by the wing!

LADY POLITIC. Burnt silk, and amber. You have muscadel
     Good i' the house –

VOLPONE.   You will not drink and part?

LADY POLITIC. No, fear not that. I doubt we shall not get
     Some English saffron – half a dram would serve;
     Your sixteen cloves, a little musk, dried mints,   60
     Bugloss, and barley-meal –

VOLPONE. [*Aside.*]   She's in again.
     Before I feigned diseases, now I have one.

LADY POLITIC. And these applied with a right scarlet cloth –

VOLPONE. [*Aside.*] Another flood of words! a very torrent!

LADY POLITIC. Shall I, sir, make you a poultice?

VOLPONE.   No, no, no.   65
     I'm very well; you need prescribe no more.

LADY POLITIC. I have, a little, studied physic; but now
     I'm all for music, save i' the forenoons
     An hour or two for painting. I would have
     A lady, indeed, t'have all letters and arts,   70
     Be able to discourse, to write, to paint,
     But principal, as Plato holds, your music –
     And so does wise Pythagoras, I take it –
     Is your true rapture, when there is concent
     In face, in voice, and clothes, and is, indeed,   75
     Our sex's chiefest ornament.

VOLPONE.   The poet
  As old in time as Plato, and as knowing,
  Says that your highest female grace is silence.

LADY POLITIC. Which o' your poets? Petrarch? or Tasso? or
      Dante?
  Guarini? Ariosto? Aretine?   80
  Cieco di Hadria? I have read them all.

VOLPONE. [*Aside.*] Is everything a cause to my destruction?

LADY POLITIC. I think I ha' two or three of 'em about me.

VOLPONE. [*Aside.*] The sun, the sea, will sooner both stand still
  Than her eternal tongue! Nothing can scape it.   85

LADY POLITIC. [*Producing a book.*] Here's *Pastor Fido* –

VOLPONE. [*Aside.*]   Profess obstinate silence;
  That's now my safest.

LADY POLITIC.   All our English writers,
  I mean such as are happy in th'Italian,
  Will deign to steal out of this author mainly;
  Almost as much as from Montaignié.   90
  He has so modern and facile a vein,
  Fitting the time, and catching the court-ear.
  Your Petrarch is more passionate, yet he,
  In days of sonneting, trusted 'em with much.
  Dante is hard, and few can understand him.   95
  But, for a desperate wit, there's Aretine!
  Only his pictures are a little obscene –
  You mark me not?

VOLPONE.   Alas, my mind's perturbed.

LADY POLITIC. Why, in such cases, we must cure ourselves,
  Make use of our philosophy –

VOLPONE.   *Ohimè.*   100

LADY POLITIC. And as we find our passions do rebel,
  Encounter 'em with reason, or divert 'em
  By giving scope unto some other humour

Of lesser danger; as in politic bodies
There's nothing more doth overwhelm the judgment   105
And clouds the understanding, than too much
Settling and fixing and, as't were, subsiding
Upon one object. For the incorporating
Of these same outward things into that part
Which we call mental, leaves some certain faeces   110
That stop the organs, and, as Plato says,
Assassinates our knowledge.

VOLPONE. [*Aside.*]   Now, the spirit
Of patience help me!

LADY POLITIC.   Come, in faith, I must
Visit you more a-days, and make you well;
Laugh and be lusty.

VOLPONE. [*Aside.*]   My good angel save me!   115

LADY POLITIC. There was but one sole man in all the world
With whom I e'er could sympathise; and he
Would lie you often three, four hours together
To hear me speak, and be sometimes so rapt,
As he would answer me quite from the purpose,   120
Like you – and you are like him, just. I'll discourse,
And 't be but only, sir, to bring you asleep,
How we did spend our time and loves together,
For some six years.

VOLPONE.   O, o, o, o, o, o.

LADY POLITIC. For we were *coaetanei*, and brought up –   125

VOLPONE. Some power, some fate, some fortune rescue me!

Act III, Scene v

[*Enter to them*] MOSCA.

[MOSCA.] God save you, madam.

LADY POLITIC.   Good sir.

VOLPONE.   Mosca? Welcome!
　Welcome to my redemption.

MOSCA.   Why, sir?

VOLPONE. [*Aside to* MOSCA.]   O,
　Rid me of this my torture quickly, there,
　My madam with the everlasting voice;
　The bells in time of pestilence ne'er made   5
　Like noise, or were in that perpetual motion!
　The cock-pit comes not near it. All my house
　But now steamed like a bath with her thick breath.
　A lawyer could not have been heard; nor scarce
　Another woman, such a hail of words   10
　She has let fall. For hell's sake, rid her hence.

MOSCA. Has she presented?

VOLPONE.   O, I do not care;
　I'll take her absence upon any price,
　With any loss.

MOSCA. [*To* LADY POLITIC.] Madam –

LADY POLITIC.   I ha' brought your patron
　A toy, a cap here, of mine own work –

MOSCA.   'Tis well.   15
　I had forgot to tell you I saw your knight
　Where you'd little think it –

LADY POLITIC.   Where?

MOSCA.   Marry,
　Where yet, if you make haste, you may appre'nd him,
　Rowing upon the water in a gondola
　With the most cunning courtesan in Venice.   20

LADY POLITIC. Is't true?

MOSCA.   Pursue 'em, and believe your eyes.
　Leave me to make your gift.

[*Exit* LADY POLITIC.]

I knew 'twould take:
For lightly, they that use themselves most license
Are still most jealous.

VOLPONE.   Mosca, hearty thanks
For thy quick fiction and delivery of me.   25
Now, to my hopes, what sayst thou?

[*Re-enter* LADY POLITIC.]

LADY POLITIC. But do you hear, sir?

VOLPONE. [*Aside*.] Again! I fear a paroxysm.

LADY POLITIC.   Which way
Rowed they together?

MOSCA.   Toward the Rialto.

LADY POLITIC. I pray you, lend me your dwarf.

MOSCA. I pray you, take him –

[*Exit* LADY POLITIC.]

Your hopes, sir, are like happy blossoms: fair,   30
And promise timely fruit, if you will stay
But the maturing; keep you at your couch.
Corbaccio will arrive straight with the will;
When he is gone, I'll tell you more. [*Exit*.]

VOLPONE.   My blood,
My spirits are returned; I am alive;
And, like your wanton gamester at primero,
Whose thought had whispered to him 'not go less',
Methinks I lie, and draw – for an encounter.

[*He draws the curtains across his bed.*]

Act III, Scene vi

MOSCA [*enters with*] BONARIO.

[MOSCA.] [*Indicating a hiding place.*] Sir, here concealed, you may
    hear all. But pray you
Have patience, sir.

One knocks.

                The same's your father knocks.
I am compelled to leave you.

[*He goes towards the knocking.*]

BONARIO.   Do so. Yet
Cannot my thought imagine this a truth.

[BONARIO *conceals himself.*]

Act III, Scene vii

MOSCA [*admits*] CORVINO [*and*] CELIA.

[MOSCA.] Death on me! You are come too soon, what meant you?
    Did not I say I would send?

CORVINO.   Yes, but I feared
You might forget it, and then they prevent us.

MOSCA. Prevent! [*Aside.*] Did e'er man haste so for his horns?
    A courtier would not ply it so for a place.   5
    [*To* CORVINO.] Well, now there's no helping it, stay here;
    I'll presently return.

[MOSCA *goes to* BONARIO.]

CORVINO.   Where are you, Celia?
You know not wherefore I have brought you hither?

CELIA. Not well, except you told me.

CORVINO.   Now I will.
    Hark hither. [*They talk apart.*]

MOSCA. [*To Bonario.*] Sir, your father hath sent word   10
    It will be half an hour ere he come;
    And therefore, if you please to walk the while
    Into that gallery – at the upper end
    There are some books to entertain the time;
    And I'll take care no man shall come unto you, sir.   15

BONARIO. Yes, I will stay there. [*Aside.*] I do doubt this fellow. [*Exit.*]

MOSCA. There, he is far enough; he can hear nothing:
    And for his father, I can keep him off.

[MOSCA *goes to* VOLPONE's *bed, opens the curtains, and whispers to him.*]

CORVINO. Nay, now, there is no starting back; and therefore
    Resolve upon it: I have so decreed.   20
    It must be done. Nor would I move't afore,
    Because I would avoid all shifts and tricks
    That might deny me.

CELIA.   Sir, let me beseech you,
    Affect not these strange trials. If you doubt
    My chastity, why, lock me up forever;   25
    Make me the heir of darkness. Let me live
    Where I may please your fears, if not your trust.

CORVINO. Believe it, I have no such humour, I.
    All that I speak I mean; yet I am not mad,
    Not horn-mad, see you? Go to, show yourself   30
    Obedient, and a wife.

CELIA.   O heaven!

CORVINO.   I say it,
    Do so.

CELIA.   Was this the train?

CORVINO.   I've told you reasons:
    What the physicians have set down; how much
    It may concern me; what my engagements are;
    My means, and the necessity of those means   35

For my recovery: wherefore, if you be
Loyal and mine, be won, respect my venture.

CELIA. Before your honour?

CORVINO.   Honour! tut, a breath.
There's no such thing in nature; a mere term
Invented to awe fools. What is my gold   40
The worse for touching? clothes for being looked on?
Why, this 's no more. An old, decrepit wretch,
That has no sense, no sinew; takes his meat
With others' fingers; only knows to gape
When you do scald his gums; a voice; a shadow;   45
And what can this man hurt you?

CELIA.   Lord! what spirit
Is this hath entered him?

CORVINO.   And for your fame,
That's such a jig; as if I would go tell it,
Cry it, on the Piazza! Who shall know it,
But he that cannot speak it, and this fellow   50
Whose lips are i' my pocket, save yourself?
If you'll proclaim't, you may! I know no other
Should come to know it.

CELIA.   Are heaven and saints then nothing?
Will they be blind, or stupid?

CORVINO.   How?

CELIA.   Good sir,
Be jealous still: emulate them, and think   55
What hate they burn with toward every sin.

CORVINO. I grant you. If I thought it were a sin
I would not urge you. Should I offer this
To some young Frenchman, or hot Tuscan blood
That had read Aretine, conned all his prints,   60
Knew every quirk within lust's labyrinth,
And were professed critic in lechery,
And I would look upon him, and applaud him,

This were a sin; but here 'tis contrary,
A pious work, mere charity, for physic,   65
And honest polity to assure mine own.

CELIA. O heaven! canst thou suffer such a change?

VOLPONE. [*Aside to* MOSCA.] Thou art mine honour, Mosca, and
    my pride,
My joy, my tickling, my delight! Go, bring 'em.   69

MOSCA. [*Advancing.*] Please you draw near, sir.

CORVINO.   Come on, what – [CELIA *resists.*]
    You will not be rebellious? By that light –

    [*He drags her to the bed.*]

MOSCA. [*To* VOLPONE.] Sir, Signor Corvino here is come to see
    you –

VOLPONE. O!

MOSCA.   And hearing of the consultation had,
    So lately, for your health, is come to offer,
    Or rather, sir, to prostitute –

CORVINO.   Thanks, sweet Mosca.   75

MOSCA. Freely, unasked, or unentreated –

CORVINO.   Well.

MOSCA. As the true, fervent instance of his love,
    His own most fair and proper wife, the beauty
    Only of price in Venice –

CORVINO.   'Tis well urged.

MOSCA. To be your comfortress, and to preserve you.   80

VOLPONE. Alas, I'm past already! Pray you, thank him
    For his good care and promptness. But, for that,
    'Tis a vain labour; e'en to fight 'gainst heaven,
    Applying fire to a stone, [*Coughing.*] uh! uh! uh! uh!
    Making a dead leaf grow again. I take   85
    His wishes gently, though; and you may tell him

What I've done for him. Marry, my state is hopeless!
Will him to pray for me, and t'use his fortune
With reverence when he comes to't.

MOSCA.   Do you hear, sir?
    Go to him with your wife.

CORVINO. [*To* CELIA.]   Heart of my father!   90
    Wilt thou persist thus? Come, I pray thee, come.
    Thou seest 'tis nothing, Celia. By this hand
    I shall grow violent. Come, do 't, I say.

CELIA. Sir, kill me rather. I will take down poison,
    Eat burning coals, do anything –

CORVINO.   Be damned!   95
    Heart! I will drag thee hence home by the hair,
    Cry thee a strumpet through the streets, rip up
    Thy mouth unto thine ears, and slit thy nose,
    Like a raw rotchet! – Do not tempt me; come,
    Yield; I am loath – Death! I will buy some slave   100
    Whom I will kill, and bind thee to him, alive;
    And at my window hang you forth, devising
    Some monstrous crime, which I, in capital letters,
    Will eat into thy flesh with *aquafortis*
    And burning cor'sives, on this stubborn breast.   105
    Now, by the blood thou hast incensed, I'll do 't!

CELIA. Sir, what you please, you may; I am your martyr.

CORVINO. Be not thus obstinate; I ha' not deserved it.
    Think who it is entreats you. Pray thee, sweet;
    Good faith, thou shalt have jewels, gowns, attires,   110
    What thou wilt, think and ask. Do but go kiss him.
    Or touch him, but. For my sake. At my suit.
    This once. [*She refuses.*] No? Not? I shall remember this.
    Will you disgrace me thus? Do you thirst my undoing?

MOSCA. Nay, gentle lady, be advised.

CORVINO.   No, no.   115
    She has watched her time. God's precious, this is scurvy,

'Tis very scurvy; and you are –

MOSCA.   Nay, good sir.

CORVINO. An errant locust, by heaven, a locust! Whore!
  Crocodile, that hast thy tears prepared,
  Expecting how thou'lt bid 'em flow.

MOSCA.   Nay, pray you, sir!   120
  She will consider.

CELIA.   Would my life would serve
  To satisfy –

CORVINO.   'Sdeath! if she would but speak to him,
  And save my reputation, 'twere somewhat;
  But spitefully to affect my utter ruin!

MOSCA. Ay, now you've put your fortune in her hands.   125
  Why, i' faith, it is her modesty, I must quit her.
  If you were absent, she would be more coming;
  I know it, and dare undertake for her.
  What woman can before her husband? Pray you,
  Let us depart and leave her here.

CORVINO.   Sweet Celia,   130
  Thou may'st redeem all yet; I'll say no more.
  If not, esteem yourself as lost.

  [*She begins to leave with him.*]

                          – Nay, stay there.

  [*Exeunt* CORVINO *and* MOSCA.]

CELIA. O God, and his good angels! whither, whither,
  Is shame fled human breasts? that with such ease
  Men dare put off your honours, and their own?   135
  Is that which ever was a cause of life
  Now placed beneath the basest circumstance,
  And modesty an exile made, for money?

  [VOLPONE] *leaps off from his couch.*

VOLPONE. Ay, in Corvino, and such earth-fed minds,

That never tasted the true heav'n of love.   140
Assure thee, Celia, he that would sell thee,
Only for hope of gain, and that uncertain,
He would have sold his part of Paradise
For ready money, had he met a copeman.
Why art thou mazed to see me thus revived?   145
Rather applaud thy beauty's miracle;
'Tis thy great work, that hath, not now alone,
But sundry times raised me in several shapes
And, but this morning, like a mountebank,
To see thee at thy window. Ay, before   150
I would have left my practice for thy love,
In varying figures I would have contended
With the blue Proteus, or the horned flood.
Now art thou welcome.

CELIA.   Sir!

VOLPONE.   Nay, fly me not.
Nor let thy false imagination   155
That I was bed-rid, make thee think I am so:
Thou shalt not find it. I am, now, as fresh,
As hot, as high, and in as jovial plight
As when in that so celebrated scene
At recitation of our comedy   160
For entertainment of the great Valois,
I acted young Antinöus, and attracted
The eyes and ears of all the ladies present,
T' admire each graceful gesture, note, and footing.

Song.

Come, my Celia, let us prove,   165
While we can, the sports of love;
Time will not be ours for ever,
He, at length, our good will sever;
Spend not then his gifts in vain.
Suns that set may rise again;   170
But if once we lose this light,
'Tis with us perpetual night.

Why should we defer our joys?
Fame and rumour are but toys.
Cannot we delude the eyes   175
Of a few poor household spies?
Or his easier ears beguile,
Thus removed by our wile?
'Tis no sin love's fruits to steal,
But the sweet thefts to reveal: 180
To be taken, to be seen,
These have crimes accounted been.

CELIA. Some serene blast me, or dire lightning strike
   This my offending face.

VOLPONE.   Why droops my Celia?
   Thou hast in place of a base husband found   185
   A worthy lover; use thy fortune well,
   With secrecy and pleasure. See, behold
   What thou art queen of;

   [*He shows her the treasure.*]

                        not in expectation,
   As I feed others, but possessed and crowned.
   See, here, a rope of pearl, and each more Orient   190
   Than that the brave Egyptian queen caroused;
   Dissolve and drink 'em. See, a carbuncle
   May put out both the eyes of our St Mark;
   A diamond would have bought Lollia Paulina
   When she came in like star-light, hid with jewels   195
   That were the spoils of provinces; take these,
   And wear, and lose 'em; yet remains an earring
   To purchase them again, and this whole state.
   A gem but worth a private patrimony
   Is nothing; we will eat such at a meal.   200
   The heads of parrots, tongues of nightingales,
   The brains of peacocks, and of ostriches
   Shall be our food, and, could we get the phoenix,
   Though nature lost her kind, she were our dish.

CELIA. Good sir, these things might move a mind affected   205

With such delights; but I, whose innocence
Is all I can think wealthy, or worth th'enjoying,
And which, once lost, I have nought to lose beyond it,
Cannot be taken with these sensual baits.
If you have conscience –

VOLPONE.   'Tis the beggar's virtue;   210
If thou hast wisdom, hear me, Celia.
Thy baths shall be the juice of July-flowers,
Spirit of roses, and of violets,
The milk of unicorns, and panthers' breath
Gathered in bags and mixed with Cretan wines.   215
Our drink shall be prepared gold and amber,
Which we will take until my roof whirl round
With the vertigo; and my dwarf shall dance,
My eunuch sing, my fool make up the antic;
Whilst we, in changed shapes, act Ovid's tales,   220
Thou like Europa now and I like Jove,
Then I like Mars and thou like Erycine;
So of the rest, till we have quite run through
And wearied all the fables of the gods.
Then will I have thee in more modern forms,   225
Attired like some sprightly dame of France,
Brave Tuscan lady, or proud Spanish beauty;
Sometimes unto the Persian Sophy's wife,
Or the Grand Signor's mistress; and, for change,
To one of our most artful courtesans,   230
Or some quick Negro, or cold Russian;
And I will meet thee in as many shapes,
Where we may so [*Kissing her.*] transfuse our wand'ring souls
Out at our lips and score up sums of pleasures,

[*He sings.*]

That the curious shall not know   235
How to tell them as they flow,
And the envious, when they find
What their number is, be pined.

CELIA. [*Struggling.*] If you have ears that will be pierced – or eyes

That can be opened – a heart may be touched –   240
Or any part that yet sounds man about you –
If you have touch of holy saints – or heaven –
Do me the grace to let me 'scape. – If not,
Be bountiful and kill me. – You do know
I am a creature hither ill betrayed   245
By one whose shame I would forget it were. –
If you will deign me neither of these graces,
Yet feed your wrath, sir, rather than your lust –
(It is a vice comes nearer manliness) –
And punish that unhappy crime of nature,   250
Which you miscall my beauty – flay my face,
Or poison it with ointments for seducing
Your blood to this rebellion. – Rub these hands
With what may cause an eating leprosy,
E'en to my bones and marrow – anything   255
That may disfavour me, save in my honour –
And I will kneel to you, pray for you, pay down
A thousand hourly vows, sir, for your health –
Report, and think you virtuous –

VOLPONE.   Think me cold,
Frozen, and impotent, and so report me?   260
That I had Nestor's hernia thou wouldst think.
I do degenerate and abuse my nation
To play with opportunity thus long.
I should have done the act, and then have parleyed.
Yield, or I'll force thee.

CELIA.   O, just God!

VOLPONE.   In vain –   265

[BONARIO] *leaps out from where* MOSCA *had placed him.*

BONARIO. Forbear, foul ravisher, libidinous swine!
Free the forced lady, or thou diest, impostor.
But that I am loath to snatch thy punishment
Out of the hand of justice, thou shouldst yet
Be made the timely sacrifice of vengeance,   270
Before this altar, and this dross, thy idol.

[*Indicates the treasure.*]

Lady, let's quit the place: it is the den
Of villainy. Fear nought, you have a guard;
And he ere long shall meet his just reward.

[*Exit with* CELIA.]

VOLPONE. Fall on me, roof, and bury me in ruin;   275
    Become my grave, that wert my shelter! O!
    I am unmasked, unspirited, undone,
    Betrayed to beggary, to infamy –

Act III, Scene viii

[*Enter to him*] MOSCA [, *bleeding*].

[MOSCA.] Where shall I run, most wretched shame of men,
    To beat out my unlucky brains?

VOLPONE.   Here, here.
    What! dost thou bleed?

MOSCA.   O, that his well-driven sword
    Had been so courteous to have cleft me down
    Unto the navel, ere I lived to see   5
    My life, my hopes, my spirits, my patron, all
    Thus desperately engaged by my error.

VOLPONE. Woe on thy fortune!

MOSCA.   And my follies, sir.

VOLPONE. Th' hast made me miserable.

MOSCA.   And myself sir.
    Who would have thought he would have hearkened so?   10

VOLPONE. What shall we do?

MOSCA.   I know not. If my heart
    Could expiate the mischance, I'd pluck it out.
    Will you be pleased to hang me, or cut my throat?

And I'll requite you, sir. Let's die like Romans,
Since we have lived like Grecians.

They knock without.

VOLPONE.   Hark! who's there?   15
  I hear some footing: officers, the *Saffi*,
  Come to apprehend us! I do feel the brand
  Hissing already at my forehead; now,
  Mine ears are boring.

MOSCA.   To your couch, sir; you
  Make that place good, however.

  [VOLPONE *lies down*.]
                      Guilty men   20
  Suspect what they deserve still.

  [*He opens the door*.]

                      Signor Corbaccio!

Act III, Scene ix

[*Enter to them*] CORBACCIO [*with* VOLTORE *behind, unseen*].

[CORBACCIO.] Why, how now, Mosca?

MOSCA.   O, undone, amazed, sir.
  Your son, I know not by what accident,
  Acquainted with your purpose to my patron
  Touching your will and making him your heir,
  Entered our house with violence, his sword drawn,   5
  Sought for you, called you wretch, unnatural,
  Vowed he would kill you.

CORBACCIO.   Me?

MOSCA.   Yes, and my patron.

CORBACCIO. This act shall disinherit him indeed.
  Here is the will.

MOSCA.   'Tis well, sir.

CORBACCIO.   Right and well.
  Be you as careful now for me.

MOSCA.   My life, sir,   10
  Is not more tendered; I am only yours.

CORBACCIO. How does he? Will he die shortly, think'st thou?

MOSCA.   I fear
  He'll outlast May.

CORBACCIO.   Today?

MOSCA.   No, last out May, sir!

CORBACCIO. Couldst thou not gi' him a dram?

MOSCA.   O, by no means, sir.

CORBACCIO. Nay, I'll not bid you.

VOLTORE. [*Aside*.]   This is a knave, I see.   15

MOSCA. [*Aside*.] How! Signor Voltore! Did he hear me?

VOLTORE.   Parasite!

MOSCA. Who's that? [*Going to* VOLTORE.] O, sir, most timely
  welcome –

VOLTORE.   Scarce
  To the discovery of your tricks, I fear.
  You are his only? And mine also? are you not?

MOSCA. Who? I, sir?

VOLTORE.   You, sir. What device is this   20
  About a will?

MOSCA.   A plot for you, sir.

VOLTORE.   Come,
  Put not your foists upon me; I shall scent 'em.

MOSCA. Did you not hear it?

VOLTORE.   Yes, I hear Corbaccio

Hath made your patron, there, his heir.

MOSCA.   'Tis true,
By my device, drawn to it by my plot,   25
With hope –

VOLTORE.   Your patron should reciprocate?
And you have promised?

MOSCA.   For your good I did, sir.
Nay, more, I told his son, brought, hid him here,
Where he might hear his father pass the deed;
Being persuaded to it by this thought, sir,   30
That the unnaturalness, first, of the act,
And then his father's oft disclaiming in him –
Which I did mean t'help on – would sure enrage him
To do some violence upon his parent.
On which the law should take sufficient hold,   35
And you be stated in a double hope.
Truth be my comfort, and my conscience,
My only aim was to dig you a fortune
Out of these two old, rotten sepulchres –

VOLTORE. I cry thee mercy, Mosca.

MOSCA.   Worth your patience   40
And your great merit, sir. And see the change!

VOLTORE. Why, what success?

MOSCA.   Most hapless! You must help, sir.
Whilst we expected th'old raven, in comes
Corvino's wife, sent hither by her husband –

VOLTORE. What, with a present?

MOSCA.   No, sir, on visitation –   45
I'll tell you how anon – and, staying long,
The youth he grows impatient, rushes forth,
Seizeth the lady, wounds me, makes her swear –
Or he would murder her, that was his vow –
T' affirm my patron to have done her rape,   50
Which how unlike it is, you see! and hence

With that pretext he's gone t'accuse his father,
Defame my patron, defeat you –

VOLTORE. Where's her husband?
Let him be sent for straight.

MOSCA.   Sir, I'll go fetch him.

VOLTORE. Bring him to the Scrutineo.

MOSCA.   Sir, I will.   55

VOLTORE. This must be stopped.

MOSCA.   O, you do nobly, sir.
Alas, 'twas laboured all, sir, for your good;
Nor was there want of counsel in the plot.
But fortune can, at any time, o'erthrow
The projects of a hundred learned clerks, sir.   60

CORBACCIO. [*Overhearing.*] What's that?

VOLTORE. [*To* CORBACCIO.]   Will 't please you, sir, to
go along?

[*Exeunt* VOLTORE *and* CORBACCIO.]

MOSCA. [*To* VOLPONE.] Patron, go in and pray for our success.

VOLPONE. [*Rising.*] Need makes devotion; heaven your labour bless!

[*Exeunt.*]

Act IV, Scene i

[*Enter* SIR] POLITIC [*and*] PEREGRINE.

[SIR POLITIC.] I told you, sir, it was a plot; you see
    What observation is! You mentioned me
    For some instructions: I will tell you, sir,
    Since we are met here in this height of Venice,
    Some few particulars I have set down   5
    Only for this meridian, fit to be known
    I will not touch, sir, at your phrase, or clothes,
    For they are old.

PEREGRINE.   Sir, I have better.

SIR POLITIC.   Pardon,
    I meant as they are themes.

PEREGRINE.   O, sir, proceed.   10
    I'll slander you no more of wit, good sir.

SIR POLITIC. First, for your garb, it must be grave and serious,
    Very reserved and locked; not tell a secret
    On any terms, not to your father; scarce
    A fable but with caution. Make sure choice   15
    Both of your company and discourse; beware
    You never speak a truth –

PEREGRINE.   How!

SIR POLITIC.   Not to strangers,
    For those be they you must converse with most;
    Others I would not know, sir, but at distance,
    So as I still might be a saver in 'em.   20
    You shall have tricks, else, passed upon you hourly.
    And then, for your religion, profess none,
    But wonder at the diversity of all;

And, for your part, protest were there no other
But simply the laws o' th' land, you could content you.   25
Nick Machiavel and Monsieur Bodin both
Were of this mind. Then must you learn the use
And handling of your silver fork at meals,
The metal of your glass – these are main matters
With your Italian – and to know the hour   30
When you must eat your melons and your figs.

PEREGRINE. Is that a point of state too?

SIR POLITIC.   Here it is;
For your Venetian, if he see a man
Preposterous in the least, he has him straight;
He has: he strips him. I'll acquaint you, sir,   35
I now have lived here, 'tis some fourteen months:
Within the first week of my landing here
All took me for a citizen of Venice,
I knew the forms so well –

PEREGRINE. [*Aside.*]   And nothing else.

SIR POLITIC. I had read Contarine, took me a house,   40
Dealt with my Jews to furnish it with movables –
Well, if I could but find one man, one man
To mine own heart, whom I durst trust, I would –

PEREGRINE. What? what, sir?

SIR POLITIC.   Make him rich, make him a fortune:
He should not think again. I would command it.   45

PEREGRINE. As how?

SIR POLITIC.   With certain projects that I have,
Which I may not discover.

PEREGRINE. [*Aside.*]   If I had
But one to wager with, I would lay odds, now,
He tells me instantly.

SIR POLITIC.   One is (and that
I care not greatly who knows) to serve the state   50

Of Venice with red herrings for three years,
And at a certain rate, from Rotterdam,
Where I have correspondence. [*Showing a letter.*] There's a letter
Sent me from one o' th' States, and to that purpose;
He cannot write his name, but that's his mark.   55

PEREGRINE. [*Examining the seal.*] He is a chandler?

SIR POLITIC.   No, a cheesemonger.
There are some other too with whom I treat
About the same negotiation,
And I will undertake it; for 'tis thus
I'll do't with ease, I've cast it all: your hoy   60
Carries but three men in her and a boy,
And she shall make me three returns a year;
So, if there come but one of three, I save,
If two, I can defalk. But this is now
If my main project fail.

PEREGRINE.   Then you have others?   65

SIR POLITIC. I should be loath to draw the subtle air
Of such a place without my thousand aims.
I'll not dissemble, sir; where'er I come,
I love to be considerative, and 'tis true
I have at my free hours thought upon   70
Some certain goods unto the state of Venice,
Which I do call my 'Cautions'; and, sir, which
I mean, in hope of pension, to propound
To the Great Council, then unto the Forty,
So to the Ten. My means are made already –   75

PEREGRINE.   By whom?

SIR POLITIC. Sir, one that, though his place b' obscure,
Yet he can sway, and they will hear him. He's
A *commandatore.*

PEREGRINE.   What, a common sergeant?

SIR POLITIC. Sir, such as they are, put it in their mouths
What they should say, sometimes, as well as greater.   80

[*Searching his pockets.*] I think I have my notes to show you –

PEREGRINE.   Good sir.

SIR POLITIC. But you shall swear unto me, on your gentry,
  Not to anticipate –

PEREGRINE.   I, sir?

SIR POLITIC.   Nor reveal
  A circumstance – My paper is not with me.

PEREGRINE. O, but you can remember, sir.

SIR POLITIC.   My first is   85
  Concerning tinder-boxes. You must know
  No family is here without its box.
  Now, sir, it being so portable a thing,
  Put case that you or I were ill affected
  Unto the state; sir, with it in our pockets,   90
  Might not I go into the Arsenalè?
  Or you? Come out again? And none the wiser?

PEREGRINE. Except yourself, sir.

SIR POLITIC.   Go to, then. I therefore
  Advertise to the state how fit it were
  That none but such as were known patriots,   95
  Sound lovers of their country, should be suffered
  T'enjoy them in their houses; and even those
  Sealed at some office, and at such a bigness
  As might not lurk in pockets.

PEREGRINE.   Admirable!

SIR POLITIC. My next is, how t'inquire, and be resolved   100
  By present demonstration, whether a ship
  Newly arrived from *Soria*, or from
  Any suspected part of all the Levant,
  Be guilty of the plague; and, where they use
  To lie out forty, fifty days, sometimes,   105
  About the Lazaretto for their trial,
  I'll save that charge and loss unto the merchant,

And in an hour clear the doubt.

PEREGRINE.   Indeed, sir?

SIR POLITIC. Or – I will lose my labour!

PEREGRINE.   My faith, that's much.

SIR POLITIC. Nay, sir, conceive me. 'Twill cost me in onions
    Some thirty *livres* –

PEREGRINE.   Which is one pound sterling.   111

SIR POLITIC. Beside my waterworks. For this I do, sir:
    First, I bring in your ship 'twixt two brick walls –
    But those the state shall venture; on the one
    I strain me a fair tarpaulin, and in that   115
    I stick my onions, cut in halves; the other
    Is full of loopholes, out at which I thrust
    The noses of my bellows; and those bellows
    I keep, with waterworks, in perpetual motion,
    (Which is the easiest matter of a hundred).   120
    Now, sir, your onion, which doth naturally
    Attract th'infection, and your bellows blowing
    The air upon him, will show instantly,
    By his changed colour, if there be contagion;
    Or else remain as fair as at the first.   125
    Now 'tis known, 'tis nothing.

PEREGRINE.   Your are right, sir.

SIR POLITIC. I would I had my note.

PEREGRINE.   Faith, so would I.
    But you ha' done well for once, sir.

SIR POLITIC. [*Searching his pockets again.*] Were I false,
    Or would be made so, I could show you reasons
    How I could sell this state to the Turk,   130
    Spite of their galleys, or their –

PEREGRINE.   Pray you, Sir Pol.

SIR POLITIC. I have 'em not about me.

PEREGRINE.   That I feared.
    They're there, sir? [*He indicates a book of* SIR POL'*s.*]

SIR POLITIC.   No, this is my diary,
    Wherein I note my actions of the day.

PEREGRINE. Pray you, let's see, sir. What is here? [*Reads.*]
        '*Notandum*   135
    A rat hath gnawn my spur leathers; notwithstanding,
    I put on new and did go forth; but first
    I threw three beans over the threshold. *Item,*
    I went and bought two toothpicks, whereof one
    I burst immediately in a discourse   140
    With a Dutch merchant 'bout *ragion' del stato.*
    From him I went and paid a *moccenigo*
    For piercing my silk stockings; by the way
    I cheapened sprats, and at St Mark's I urined.'
    Faith, these are politic notes!

SIR POLITIC.   Sir, I do slip   145
    No action of my life, thus, but I quote it.

PEREGRINE. Believe me, it is wise!

SIR POLITIC.   Nay, sir, read forth.

Act IV, Scene ii

[*Enter to them*] LADY [POL,] NANO [, *and the two*] WOMEN.

[LADY POLITIC.] Where should this loose knight be, trow?
    Sure, he's housed.

NANO. Why, then he's fast.

LADY POLITIC.   Ay, he plays both with me.
    I pray you stay. This heat will do more harm
    To my complexion than his heart is worth.
    I do not care to hinder, but to take him. –   5
    How it comes off! [*Rubbing her cheeks.*]

1 WOMAN. [*Pointing.*] My master's yonder.

LADY POLITIC.   Where?

2 WOMAN. With a young gentleman.

LADY POLITIC.   That same's the party!
   In man's apparel. [*To* NANO.] Pray you, sir, jog my knight.
   I will be tender to his reputation,
   However he demerit.

SIR POLITIC. [*Seeing her.*] My lady!

PEREGRINE.   Where?   10

SIR POLITIC. 'Tis she indeed; sir, you shall know her. She is,
   Were she not mine, a lady of that merit
   For fashion and behaviour, and for beauty,
   I durst compare –

PEREGRINE.   It seems you are not jealous,
   That dare commend her.

SIR POLITIC.   Nay, and for discourse –   15

PEREGRINE. Being your wife, she cannot miss that.

SIR POLITIC. [*Introducing* PEREGRINE.]   Madam,
   Here is a gentleman; pray you, use him fairly.
   He seems a youth, but he is –

LADY POLITIC.   None?

SIR POLITIC.   Yes, one
   Has put his face as soon into the world –

LADY POLITIC. You mean, as early? But today?

SIR POLITIC.   How's this!   20

LADY POLITIC. Why, in this habit, sir; you apprehend me.
   Well, Master Would-be, this doth not become you.
   I had thought the odour, sir, of your good name
   Had been more precious to you; that you would not
   Have done this dire massacre on your honour;   25
   One of your gravity, and rank besides!

But knights, I see, care little for the oath
They make to ladies, chiefly their own ladies.   29

SIR POLITIC. Now, by my spurs, the symbol of my knighthood –

PEREGRINE. [*Aside.*] Lord, how his brain is humbled for an oath!

SIR POLITIC. I reach you not.

LADY POLITIC.   Right, sir, your polity
May bear it through thus. [*To* PEREGRINE.] Sir, a word with you.
I would be loath to contest publicly
With any gentlewoman, or to seem
Froward, or violent: as *The Courtier* says,   35
It comes too near rusticity in a lady,
Which I would shun by all means. And, however
I may deserve from Master Would-be, yet
T'have one fair gentlewoman thus be made
Th'unkind instrument to wrong another,   40
And one she knows not, ay, and to persever,
In my poor judgment is not warranted
From being a solecism in our sex,
If not in manners.

PEREGRINE.   How is this?

SIR POLITIC.   Sweet madam,
Come nearer to your aim.

LADY POLITIC.   Marry, and will, sir.   45
Since you provoke me with your impudence
And laughter of your light land-siren here,
Your Sporus, your hermaphrodite –

PEREGRINE.   What's here?
Poetic fury and historic storms!

SIR POLITIC. The gentleman, believe it, is of worth,   50
And of our nation.

LADY POLITIC.   Ay, your Whitefriars nation!
Come, I blush for you, Master Would-be, ay;
And am ashamed you should ha' no more forehead

Than thus to be the patron, or St George,
To a lewd harlot, a base fricatrice,   55
A female devil in a male outside.

SIR POLITIC. [*To* PEREGRINE.] Nay,
And you be such a one, I must bid adieu,
To your delights. The case appears too liquid.

[*Exit* SIR POLITIC.]

LADY POLITIC. Ay, you may carry't clear, with your state-face!
But for your carnival concupiscence,   60
Who here is fled for liberty of conscience
From furious persecution of the marshal,
Her will I disple.

PEREGRINE. This is fine, i' faith!
And do you use this often? Is this part
Of your wit's exercise, 'gainst you have occasion?   65
Madam –

LADY POLITIC. Go to, sir.

PEREGRINE.   Do you hear me, lady?
Why, if your knight have set you to beg shirts,
Or to invite me home, you might have done it
A nearer way by far.

LADY POLITIC.   This cannot work you
Out of my snare.

PEREGRINE.   Why, am I in it, then?   70
Indeed, your husband told me you were fair,
And so you are; only your nose inclines,
That side that's next the sun, to the queen-apple.

LADY POLITIC. This cannot be endured by any patience.

Act IV, Scene iii

[*Enter to them*] MOSCA.

[MOSCA.] What's the matter, madam?

LADY POLITIC.   If the Senate
  Right not my quest in this, I will protest 'em
  To all the world no aristocracy.

MOSCA.   What is the injury, lady?

LADY POLITIC. Why, the callet
  You told me of, here I have ta'en disguised.   5

MOSCA. Who? This! What means your ladyship? The creature
  I mentioned to you is apprehended now
  Before the Senate. You shall see her –

LADY POLITIC.   Where?

MOSCA. I'll bring you to her. This young gentleman,
  I saw him land this morning at the port.   10

LADY POLITIC. Is 't possible? How has my judgment wandered!
  Sir, I must, blushing, say to you I have erred,
  And plead your pardon!

PEREGRINE.   What, more changes yet?

LADY POLITIC. I hope y' ha' not the malice to remember
  A gentlewoman's passion. If you stay   15
  In Venice here, please you to use me, sir –

MOSCA. Will you go, madam?

LADY POLITIC.   Pray you, sir, use me. In faith,
  The more you see me, the more I shall conceive,
  You have forgot our quarrel.

  [*Exeunt* LADY POL, MOSCA, NANO, *and* WOMEN.]

PEREGRINE.   This is rare!
  Sir Politic Would-be? – no, Sir Politic Bawd!   20
  To bring me thus acquainted with his wife!
  Well, wise Sir Pol, since you have practised thus

Upon my freshmanship, I'll try your salt-head,
What proof it is against a counter-plot. [*Exit.*]

Act IV, Scene iv

[*Enter*] VOLTORE, CORBACCIO, CORVINO, [*and*] MOSCA.

[VOLTORE.] Well, now you know the carriage of the business,
    Your constancy is all that is required
    Unto the safety of it.

MOSCA.   Is the lie
    Safely conveyed amongst us? Is that sure?
    Knows every man his burden?

CORVINO.   Yes.

MOSCA.   Then shrink not.   5

CORVINO. [*Aside to* MOSCA.] But knows the advocate the truth?

MOSCA.   O, sir,
    By no means. I devised a formal tale
    That salved your reputation. But be valiant, sir.

CORVINO. I fear no one but him, that this his pleading
    Should make him stand for a co-heir –

MOSCA.   Co-halter,   10
    Hang him! We will but use his tongue, his noise,
    As we do Croaker's here. [*Indicates* CORBACCIO.]

CORVINO.   Ay, what shall he do?

MOSCA. When we ha' done, you mean?

CORVINO.   Yes.

MOSCA.   Why, we'll think:
    Sell him for mummia, he's half dust already.

    To VOLTORE [*aside, indicating* CORVINO].

Do you not smile to see this buffalo,   15

How he doth sport it with his head? [*To himself.*] I should,
If all were well and past. [*To* CORBACCIO.] Sir, only you
Are he that shall enjoy the crop of all,
And these not know for whom they toil.

CORBACCIO. Ay, peace!

MOSCA. [*To* CORVINO.] – But you shall eat it!
  [*To himself.*] Much! – [*And then to Voltore again.*] Worshipful sir,   20
  Mercury sit upon your thund'ring tongue,
  Or the French Hercules, and make your language
  As conquering as his club, to beat along,
  As with a tempest, flat, our adversaries –
  [*To him aside.*] But much more yours, sir.

VOLTORE.   Here they come, ha' done.

MOSCA. I have another witness if you need, sir,   26
  I can produce.

VOLTORE.   Who is it?

MOSCA.   Sir, I have her.

Act IV, Scene v
[*Enter to them*] *four* AVOCATORI, BONARIO, CELIA, NOTARIO,
COMMANDATORI [, *and other* COURT OFFICIALS].

[1 AVOCATORE.] The like of this the Senate never heard of.

2 AVOCATORE. 'Twill come most strange to them when we report it.

4 AVOCATORE. The gentlewoman has been ever held
  Of unreproved name.

3 AVOCATORE.   So the young man.

4 AVOCATORE. The more unnatural part that of the father.   5

2 AVOCATORE. More of the husband.

1 AVOCATORE.   I not know to give
  His act a name, it is so monstrous!

4 AVOCATORE. But the impostor, he is a thing created
   T'exceed example!

[1] AVOCATORE.   And all after-times!

2 AVOCATORE. I never heard a true voluptuary
   Described but him.   10

3 AVOCATORE.   Appear yet those were cited?

NOTARIO. All but the old magnifico, Volpone.

1 AVOCATORE. Why is not he here?

MOSCA.   Please your fatherhoods,
   Here is his advocate. Himself's so weak,
   So feeble –

4 AVOCATORE. What are you?

BONARIO.   His parasite,   15
   His knave, his pander! I beseech the court
   He may be forced to come, that your grave eyes
   May bear strong witness of his strange impostures.

VOLTORE. Upon my faith and credit with your virtues,
   He is not able to endure the air.   20

2 AVOCATORE. Bring him, however.

3 AVOCATORE.   We will see him.

4 AVOCATORE.   Fetch him.

   [*Exeunt* OFFICERS.]

VOLTORE. Your fatherhoods' fit pleasures be obeyed,
   But sure the sight will rather move your pities
   Than indignation. May it please the court,
   In the mean time, he may be heard in me.   25
   I know this place most void of prejudice,
   And therefore crave it, since we have no reason
   To fear our truth should hurt our cause.

3 AVOCATORE.   Speak free.

VOLTORE. Then know, most honoured fathers, I must now

Discover to your strangely abused ears   30
The most prodigious and most frontless piece
Of solid impudence and treachery
That ever vicious nature yet brought forth
To shame the state of Venice.

[*Indicating* CELIA.]
                              This lewd woman,
That wants no artificial looks or tears   35
To help the visor she has now put on,
Hath long been known a close adulteress
To that lascivious youth there;

[*Indicating* BONARIO.]

                              not suspected,
I say, but known, and taken, in the act,
With him; and by this man, the easy husband

[*Indicating* CORVINO.]   40

Pardoned; whose timeless bounty makes him now
Stand here, the most unhappy, innocent person
That ever man's own goodness made accused.
For these, not knowing how to owe a gift
Of that dear grace but with their shame, being placed   45
So above all powers of their gratitude,
Began to hate the benefit, and in place
Of thanks, devise t'extirp the memory
Of such an act. Wherein I pray your fatherhoods
T'observe the malice, yea, the rage of creatures   50
Discovered in their evils; and what heart
Such take, even from their crimes. But that anon
Will more appear. This gentleman, the father,

[*Indicating* CORBACCIO.]

Hearing of this foul fact, with many others
Which daily struck at his too tender ears,   55
And grieved in nothing more than that he could not
Preserve himself a parent (his son's ills
Growing to that strange flood) at last decreed

To disinherit him.

1 AVOCATORE.   These be strange turns!   59

2 AVOCATORE. The young man's fame was ever fair and honest.

VOLTORE. So much more full of danger is his vice,
        That can beguile so under shade of virtue.
        But, as I said, my honoured sires, his father
        Having this settled purpose (by what means
        To him betrayed, we know not), and this day   65
        Appointed for the deed, that parricide
        (I cannot style him better), by confederacy
        Preparing this his paramour to be there,
        Entered Volpone's house (who was the man,
        Your fatherhoods must understand, designed   70
        For the inheritance), there sought his father.
        But with what purpose sought he him, my lords?
        I tremble to pronounce it, that a son
        Unto a father, and to such a father,
        Should have so foul, felonious intent: 75
        It was, to murder him! When, being prevented
        By his more happy absence, what then did he?
        Not check his wicked thoughts; no, now new deeds,
        (Mischief doth ever end where it begins)
        An act of horror, fathers! He dragged forth   80
        The aged gentleman, that had there lain bed-rid
        Three years and more, out of his innocent couch,
        Naked, upon the floor, there left him; wounded
        His servant in the face; and, with this strumpet,
        The stale to his forged practice, who was glad   85
        To be so active (I shall here desire
        Your fatherhoods to note but my collections,
        As most remarkable), thought at once to stop
        His father's ends, discredit his free choice
        In the old gentleman, redeem themselves   90
        By laying infamy upon this man,
        To whom, with blushing, they should owe their lives.

1 AVOCATORE. What proofs have you of this?

BONARIO.   Most honoured fathers,
  I humbly crave there be no credit given
  To this man's mercenary tongue.

2 AVOCATORE.   Forbear.   95

BONARIO. His soul moves in his fee.

3 AVOCATORE.   O, sir!

BONARIO.   This fellow,
  For six sols more, would plead against his Maker.

1 AVOCATORE. You do forget yourself.

VOLTORE.   Nay, nay, grave fathers,
  Let him have scope. Can any man imagine
  That he will spare's accuser, that would not   100
  Have spared his parent?

1 AVOCATORE.   Well, produce your proofs.

CELIA. I would I could forget I were a creature!

VOLTORE. Signor Corbaccio!

4 AVOCATORE.   What is he?

VOLTORE.   The father.

2 AVOCATORE. Has he had an oath?

NOTARIO.   Yes.

CORBACCIO.   What must I do now?

NOTARIO. Your testimony's craved.

CORBACCIO. [*Mishearing.*]   Speak to the knave?   105
  I'll ha' my mouth first stopped with earth. My heart
  Abhors his knowledge; I disclaim in him.

1 AVOCATORE. But for what cause?

CORBACCIO.   The mere portent of nature.
  He is an utter stranger to my loins.

BONARIO. Have they made you to this?

CORBACCIO.   I will not hear thee,   110
  Monster of men, swine, goat, wolf, parricide!
  Speak not, thou viper.

BONARIO.   Sir, I will sit down,
  And rather wish my innocence should suffer,
  Than I resist the authority of a father.

VOLTORE. Signor Corvino!

2 AVOCATORE.   This is strange!

1 AVOCATORE.   Who's this?   115

NOTARIO. The husband.

4 AVOCATORE.   Is he sworn?

NOTARIO.   He is.

3 AVOCATORE.   Speak, then.

CORVINO. This woman, please your fatherhoods, is a whore
  Of most hot exercise, more than a partridge,
  Upon record –

1 AVOCATORE. No more.

CORVINO.   Neighs like a jennet.

NOTARIO. Preserve the honour of the court.

CORVINO.   I shall,   120
  And modesty of your most reverend ears.
  And yet I hope that I may say these eyes
  Have seen her glued unto that piece of cedar,
  That fine, well-timbered gallant; and that here

  [*Indicating his forehead.*]

  The letters may be read, thorough the horn,   125
  That make the story perfect.

MOSCA. [*Aside to* CORVINO.] Excellent, sir!

CORVINO. [*Aside to* MOSCA.] There is no shame in this, now, is
    there?

MOSCA.   None.

CORVINO. [*To the Court.*] Or if I said I hoped that she were onward
 To her damnation, if there be a hell
 Greater than whore and woman; a good Catholic   130
 May make the doubt.

3 AVOCATORE.   His grief hath made him frantic.

1 AVOCATORE. Remove him hence.

 [CELIA] *swoons.*

2 AVOCATORE.

        Look to the woman.

CORVINO.   Rare!
 Prettily feigned! Again!

4 AVOCATORE.   Stand from about her.

1 AVOCATORE. Give her the air.

3 AVOCATORE. [*To* MOSCA.] What can you say?

MOSCA.   My wound,
 May't please your wisdoms, speaks for me, received 135
 In aid of my good patron, when he missed
 His sought-for father, when that well-taught dame
 Had her cue given her to cry out a rape.

BONARIO. O most laid impudence! Fathers –

3 AVOCATORE.   Sir, be silent,
 You had your hearing free, so must they theirs. 140

2 AVOCATORE. I do begin to doubt th'imposture here.

4 AVOCATORE. This woman has too many moods.

VOLTORE.   Grave fathers,
 She is a creature of a most professed
 And prostituted lewdness.

CORVINO.   Most impetuous,
 Unsatisfied, grave fathers!

VOLTORE.   May her feignings   145
  Not take your wisdoms; but this day she baited
  A stranger, a grave knight, with her loose eyes
  And more lascivious kisses. [*Indicating* MOSCA.] This man saw 'em
  Together on the water in a gondola.

MOSCA. Here is the lady herself that saw 'em too,   150
  Without; who then had in the open streets
  Pursued them, but for saving of her knight's honour.

1 AVOCATORE. Produce that lady.

2 AVOCATORE.   Let her come.

  [*Exit* MOSCA.]

4 AVOCATORE.   These things,
  They strike with wonder!

3 AVOCATORE.   I am turned a stone!

Act IV, Scene vi

[*Enter to them*] MOSCA [*with*] LADY [POL].

[MOSCA.] Be resolute, madam.

LADY POLITIC. [*Indicating* CELIA.] Ay, this same is she.
  Out, thou chameleon harlot! Now thine eyes
  Vie tears with the hyena. Darest thou look
  Upon my wronged face? [*To* AVOCATORI.] I cry your pardons:
  I fear I have forgettingly transgressed   5
  Against the dignity of the court –

2 AVOCATORE.   No, madam.

LADY POLITIC. And been exorbitant –

2 AVOCATORE.   You have not, lady.

4 AVOCATORE. These proofs are strong.

LADY POLITIC.   Surely, I had no purpose
  To scandalise your honours, or my sex's.

3 AVOCATORE. We do believe it.

LADY POLITIC.   Surely, you may believe it.   10

2 AVOCATORE. Madam, we do.

LADY POLITIC.   Indeed, you may; my breeding
   Is not so coarse –

4 AVOCATORE.   We know it.

LADY POLITIC.   To offend
   With pertinancy –

3 AVOCATORE.   Lady –

LADY POLITIC.   Such a presence;
   No, surely.

1 AVOCATORE. We well think it.

LADY POLITIC.   You may think it.

1 AVOCATORE. Let her o'ercome. [*To* BONARIO.] What
   witnesses have you   15
   To make good your report?

BONARIO.   Our consciences.

CELIA. And heaven, that never fails the innocent.

4 AVOCATORE. These are no testimonies.

BONARIO.   Not in your courts,
   Where multitude and clamour overcomes.

1 AVOCATORE. Nay, then you do wax insolent.

   VOLPONE *is brought in, as impotent.* [LADY POL *embraces him.*]

VOLTORE.   Here, here,   20
   The testimony comes that will convince,
   And put to utter dumbness their bold tongues.
   See here, grave fathers, here's the ravisher,
   The rider on men's wives, the great impostor,
   The grand voluptuary! Do you not think   25
   These limbs should affect venery? Or these eyes

Covet a concubine? Pray you, mark these hands:
Are they not fit to stroke a lady's breasts?
Perhaps he doth dissemble?

BONARIO.   So he does.   29

VOLTORE. Would you ha' him tortured?

BONARIO.   I would have him proved.

VOLTORE. Best try him, then, with goads, or burning irons;
    Put him to the *strappado*. I have heard
    The rack hath cured the gout. Faith, give it him,
    And help him of a malady; be courteous.
    I'll undertake, before these honoured fathers,   35
    He shall have yet as many left diseases
    As she has known adulterers, or thou strumpets.
    O, my most equal hearers, if these deeds,
    Acts of this bold and most exorbitant strain,
    May pass with sufferance, what one citizen   40
    But owes the forfeit of his life, yea, fame,
    To him that dares traduce him? Which of you
    Are safe, my honoured fathers? I would ask,
    With leave of your grave fatherhoods, if their plot
    Have any face or colour like to truth?   45
    Or if, unto the dullest nostril here,
    It smell not rank and most abhorred slander?
    I crave your care of this good gentleman,
    Whose life is much endangered by their fable;
    And as for them, I will conclude with this: 50
    That vicious persons when they're hot and fleshed
    In impious acts, their constancy abounds:
    Damned deeds are done with greatest confidence.

1 AVOCATORE. Take 'em to custody, and sever them.

[CELIA *and* BONARIO *are led out separately.*]

2 AVOCATORE. 'Tis pity two such prodigies should live.   55

1 AVOCATORE. Let the old gentleman be returned with care.
    I'm sorry our credulity wronged him.

[*Exeunt* OFFICERS *with* VOLPONE.]

4 AVOCATORE. These are two creatures!

3 AVOCATORE.   I have an earthquake in me!

2 AVOCATORE. Their shame, even in their cradles, fled their
    faces.

4 AVOCATORE. [*To* VOLTORE.] You've done a worthy service
    to the state, sir,   60
    In their discovery.

2 AVOCATORE.   You shall hear ere night
    What punishment the court decrees upon 'em.

VOLTORE. We thank your fatherhoods.

    [*Exeunt* AVOCATORI, NOTARIO, COMMANDATORI, *and*
    other COURT OFFICIALS.]

                           How like you it?

MOSCA.   Rare.
    I'd ha' your tongue, sir, tipped with gold for this;
    I'd ha' you be the heir to the whole city;   65
    The earth I'd have want men, ere you want living.
    They're bound t'erect your statue in St Mark's.
    Signor Corvino, I would have you go
    And show yourself, that you have conquered.

CORVINO.   Yes.   69

MOSCA. [*Aside to him.*] It was much better that you should profess
    Yourself a cuckold thus, than that the other
    Should have been proved.

CORVINO.   Nay, I considered that:
    Now, it is her fault.

MOSCA.   Then, it had been yours.

CORVINO. True. I do doubt this advocate still.

MOSCA.   I' faith,
    You need not; I dare ease you of that care.   75

CORVINO. I trust thee, Mosca.

MOSCA.   As your own soul, sir.

   [*Exit* CORVINO.]

CORBACCIO. Mosca!

MOSCA. [*Going to him*.] Now for your business, sir.

CORBACCIO.   How! Ha' you business?

MOSCA. Yes, yours, sir.

CORBACCIO.   O, none else?

MOSCA.   None else, not I.

CORBACCIO. Be careful then.

MOSCA.   Rest you with both your eyes, sir.

CORBACCIO. Dispatch it.

MOSCA.   Instantly.

CORBACCIO.   And look that all,   80
   Whatever, be put in: jewels, plate, moneys,
   Household stuff, bedding, curtains.

MOSCA.   Curtain-rings, sir.
   Only the advocate's fee must be deducted.

CORBACCIO. I'll pay him now; you'll be too prodigal.

MOSCA. Sir, I must tender it.

CORBACCIO.   Two *chequins* is well?   85

MOSCA. No, six, sir.

CORBACCIO.   'Tis too much.

MOSCA.   He talked a great while;
   You must consider that, sir.

CORBACCIO. [*Giving money*.] Well, there's three –

MOSCA. I'll give it him.

CORBACCIO.   Do so, and there's for thee. [*Exit*.]

MOSCA. [*Aside.*] Bountiful bones! What horrid, strange offence
   Did he commit 'gainst nature in his youth,   90
   Worthy this age? [*To* VOLTORE.] You see, sir, how I work
   Unto your ends; take you no notice.

VOLTORE.   No,
   I'll leave you.

MOSCA.   All is yours,

   [*Exit* VOLTORE.]

                 – the devil and all,
   Good advocate! [*To* LADY POL.] Madam, I'll bring you home.

LADY POLITIC. No, I'll go see your patron.

MOSCA.   That you shall not. 95
   I'll tell you why: my purpose is to urge
   My patron to reform his will, and for
   The zeal you've shown today, whereas before
   You were but third or fourth, you shall be now
   Put in the first; which would appear as begged   100
   If you were present. Therefore –

LADY POLITIC.   You shall sway me.

   [*Exeunt.*]

Act V, Scene i

[*Enter*] VOLPONE.

[VOLPONE.] Well, I am here, and all this brunt is passed.
   I ne'er was in dislike with my disguise
   Till this fled moment. Here 'twas good, in private;
   But in your public – *cavè* whilst I breathe.
   'Fore God, my left leg 'gan to have the cramp,   5
   And I appre'nded straight some power had struck me
   With a dead palsy. Well, I must be merry
   And shake it off. A many of these fears
   Would put me into some villainous disease,
   Should they come thick upon me. I'll prevent 'em.   10
   Give me a bowl of lusty wine to fright
   This humour from my heart. Hum, hum, hum!

He drinks.

'Tis almost gone already; I shall conquer.
   Any device, now, of rare, ingenious knavery
   That would possess me with a violent laughter,   15
   Would make me up again. So, so, so, so.

Drinks again.

This heat is life; 'tis blood by this time! Mosca!

Act V, Scene ii

[*Enter to him*] MOSCA.

[MOSCA.] How now, sir? Does the day look clear again?
   Are we recovered? and wrought out of error
   Into our way? to see our path before us?

Is our trade free once more?

VOLPONE.   Exquisite Mosca!

MOSCA. Was it not carried learnedly?

VOLPONE.   And stoutly.   5
    Good wits are greatest in extremities.

MOSCA. It were a folly beyond thought to trust
    Any grand act unto a cowardly spirit.
    You are not taken with it enough, methinks?

VOLPONE. O, more than if I had enjoyed the wench: 10
    The pleasure of all womankind's not like it.

MOSCA. Why, now you speak, sir! We must here be fixed;
    Here we must rest. This is our masterpiece;
    We cannot think to go beyond this.

VOLPONE.   True,
    Th' ast played thy prize, my precious Mosca.

MOSCA.   Nay, sir,   15
    To gull the court –

VOLPONE.   And quite divert the torrent
    Upon the innocent.

MOSCA.   Yes, and to make
    So rare a music out of discords –

VOLPONE.   Right.
    That yet to me's the strangest! how th'ast borne it,
    That these, being so divided 'mongst themselves,   20
    Should not scent somewhat, or in me or thee,
    Or doubt their own side.

MOSCA.   True. They will not see't;
    Too much light blinds 'em, I think. Each of 'em
    Is so possessed and stuffed with his own hopes
    That anything unto the contrary,   25
    Never so true, or never so apparent,
    Never so palpable, they will resist it –

VOLPONE. Like a temptation of the devil.

MOSCA   Right, sir.
   Merchants may talk of trade, and your great signors
   Of land that yields well; but if Italy   30
   Have any glebe more fruitful than these fellows,
   I am deceived. Did not your advocate rare?

VOLPONE. O – 'My most honoured fathers, my grave fathers,
   Under correction of your fatherhoods,
   What face of truth is here? If these strange deeds   35
   May pass, most honoured fathers' – I had much ado
   To forbear laughing.

MOSCA.   'T seemed to me you sweat, sir.

VOLPONE. In troth, I did a little.

MOSCA. But confess, sir, Were you not daunted?

VOLPONE.   In good faith, I was
   A little in a mist, but not dejected;   40
   Never but still myself.

MOSCA.   I think it, sir.
   Now, so truth help me, I must needs say this, sir,
   And out of conscience, for your advocate:
   He's taken pains, in faith, sir, and deserved,
   In my poor judgment (I speak it under favour,   45
   Not to contrary you, sir), very richly –
   Well – to be cozened.

VOLPONE.   Troth, and I think so too,
   By that I heard him in the latter end.

MOSCA. O, but before, sir; had you heard him first
   Draw it to certain heads, then aggravate,   50
   Then use his vehement figures – I looked still
   When he would shift a shirt; and doing this
   Out of pure love, no hope of gain –

VOLPONE.   'Tis right.
   I cannot answer him, Mosca, as I would,

Not yet; but for thy sake, at thy entreaty,   55
I will begin e'en now to vex 'em all,
This very instant.

MOSCA.   Good, sir.

VOLPONE.   Call the dwarf
And eunuch forth.

MOSCA.   Castrone! Nano!

[*Enter* CASTRONE *and* NANO.]

NANO.   Here.

VOLPONE. Shall we have a jig now?

MOSCA.   What you please, sir.

VOLPONE. Go, straight give out about the streets, you two,   60
That I am dead; do it with constancy,
Sadly, do your hear? Impute it to the grief
Of this late slander.

[*Exeunt* CASTRONE *and* NANO.]

MOSCA.   What do you mean, sir?

VOLPONE.   O,
I shall have instantly my vulture, crow,
Raven, come flying hither on the news   65
To peck for carrion, my she-wolf and all,
Greedy and full of expectation –

MOSCA. And then to have it ravished from their mouths?

VOLPONE. 'Tis true. I will ha' thee put on a gown,
And take upon thee as thou wert mine heir;   70
Show 'em a will. Open that chest and reach
Forth one of those that has the blanks. I'll straight
Put in thy name.

MOSCA. [*Getting him a blank will.*] It will be rare, sir.

VOLPONE.   Ay,
When they e'en gape, and find themselves deluded –

MOSCA. Yes.

VOLPONE.   And thou use them scurvily. Dispatch.   75
　　Get on thy gown.

MOSCA. [*Dressing.*] But what, sir, if they ask
　　After the body?

VOLPONE.   Say it was corrupted.

MOSCA. I'll say it stunk, sir; and was fain t'have it
　　Coffined up instantly and sent away.

VOLPONE. Anything; what thou wilt. Hold, here's my will.   80
　　Get thee a cap, a count-book, pen and ink,
　　Papers afore thee; sit as thou wert taking
　　An inventory of parcels. I'll get up
　　Behind the curtain, on a stool, and hearken;
　　Sometime peep over, see how they do look,   85
　　With what degrees their blood doth leave their faces.
　　O, 'twill afford me a rare meal of laughter.

MOSCA. Your advocate will turn stark dull upon it.

VOLPONE. It will take off his oratory's edge.

MOSCA. But your *clarissimo*, old round-back, he   90
　　Will crump you like a hog-louse with the touch.

VOLPONE. And what Corvino?

MOSCA.   O, sir, look for him
　　Tomorrow morning with a rope and dagger
　　To visit all the streets: he must run mad.
　　My lady too, that came into the court   95
　　To bear false witness for your worship.

VOLPONE.   Yes,
　　And kissed me 'fore the fathers, when my face
　　Flowed all with oils –

MOSCA.   And sweat – sir. Why, your gold
　　Is such another med'cine, it dries up
　　All those offensive savours. It transforms   100

The most deformed, and restores 'em lovely
As 'twere the strange poetical girdle. Jove
Could not invent t'himself a shroud more subtle
To pass Acrisius' guards. It is the thing
Makes all the world her grace, her youth, her beauty.   105

VOLPONE. I think she loves me.

MOSCA.   Who? The lady, sir?
She's jealous of you.

VOLPONE.   Dost thou say so?

[*Knocking without.*]

MOSCA.   Hark,
There's some already.

VOLPONE.   Look.

MOSCA. [*Looking out.*]   It is the vulture;   109
He has the quickest scent.

VOLPONE.   I'll to my place,
Thou to thy posture. [*He conceals himself.*]

MOSCA.   I am set.

VOLPONE.   But, Mosca,
Play the artificer now; torture 'em rarely.

Act V, Scene iii

[*Enter to them*] VOLTORE.

[VOLTORE.] How now, my Mosca?

MOSCA. [*Writing.*]   *Turkey carpets, nine –*

VOLTORE. Taking an inventory? That is well.

MOSCA. *Two suits of bedding, tissue –*

VOLTORE.   Where's the will?
Let me read that the while.

[*Enter Servants, carrying* CORBACCIO *in a chair.*]

CORBACCIO.   So, set me down,
And get you home.

   [*Exeunt* SERVANTS.]

VOLTORE.   Is he come now, to trouble us?   5

MOSCA. *Of cloth of gold, two more –*

CORBACCIO.   Is it done, Mosca?

MOSCA. *Of several velvets, eight –*

VOLTORE.   I like his care.

CORBACCIO. Dost thou not hear?

   [*Enter* CORVINO.]

CORVINO.   Ha! Is th' hour come,
Mosca?

   VOLPONE *peeps from behind a traverse.*

VOLPONE. [*Aside.*] Ay, now they muster.

CORVINO.   What does the advocate here,
Or this Corbaccio?

CORBACCIO.   What do these here?

   [*Enter* LADY POL.]

LADY POLITIC.   Mosca!   10
Is his thread spun?

MOSCA.   *Eight chests of linen –*

VOLPONE. [*Aside.*]   O,
My fine Dame Would-be too!

CORVINO.   Mosca, the will,
That I may show it these and rid 'em hence.

MOSCA. *Six chests of diaper, four of damask –*
                              There.

[*He gives* CORVINO *the will.*]

CORBACCIO. Is that the will?

MOSCA.   *Down-beds and bolsters* –

VOLPONE. [*Aside.*]   Rare!
  Be busy still. Now they begin to flutter;   15
  They never think of me. Look, see, see, see!
  How their swift eyes run over the long deed
  Unto the name, and to the legacies,
  What is bequeathed them there –

MOSCA.   *Ten suits of hangings* –   20

VOLPONE. [*Aside.*] Ay, i' their garters, Mosca. Now their hopes
  Are at the gasp.

VOLTORE.   Mosca the heir!

CORBACCIO.   What's that?

VOLPONE. [*Aside.*] My advocate is dumb. Look to my merchant:
  He has heard of some strange storm, a ship is lost,
  He faints. My lady will swoon. Old glazen-eyes,   25
  He hath not reached his despair yet.

CORBACCIO. [*Getting possession of the will.*] All these
  Are out of hope; I'm sure the man.

CORVINO.   But Mosca –

MOSCA. *Two cabinets* –

CORVINO.   Is this in earnest?

MOSCA.   *One*
  Of ebony –

CORVINO.   Or do you but delude me

MOSCA. *The other, mother of pearl* – I am very busy.   30
  Good faith, it is a fortune thrown upon me –
  Item, one salt of agate – not my seeking.

LADY POLITIC. Do you hear, sir?

MOSCA.   *A perfumed box* – Pray you forbear,
    You see I am troubled – *made of an onyx* –

LADY POLITIC.   How?

MOSCA. Tomorrow, or next day, I shall be at leisure   35
    To talk with you all.

CORVINO.   Is this my large hope's issue?

LADY POLITIC. Sir, I must have a fairer answer.

MOSCA.   Madam!
    Marry, and shall: pray you, fairly quit my house.
    Nay, raise no tempest with your looks; but hark you:
    Remember what your ladyship offered me   40
    To put you in an heir; go to, think on't;
    And what you said e'en your best madams did
    For maintenance, and why not you? Enough!
    Go home and use the poor Sir Pol, your knight, well,
    For fear I tell some riddles. Go, be melancholic.   45

    [*Exit* LADY POL.]

VOLPONE. [*Aside.*] O, my fine devil!

CORVINO.   Mosca, pray you a word.

MOSCA. Lord! Will not you take your dispatch hence yet?
    Methinks, of all, you should have been th'example.
    Why should you stay here? With what thought? What promise?
    Hear you: do not you know I know you an ass?   50
    And that you would most fain have been a wittol
    If fortune would have let you? That you are
    A declared cuckold, on good terms? This pearl
    You'll say was yours? Right. This diamond?
    I'll not deny't, but thank you. Much here else?   55
    It may be so. Why, think that these good works
    May help to hide your bad. I'll not betray you,
    Although you be but extraordinary,
    And have it only in title, it sufficeth.
    Go home, be melancholic too, or mad.   60

[*Exit* CORVINO.]

VOLPONE. [*Aside.*] Rare, Mosca! How his villainy becomes him!

VOLTORE. Certain he doth delude all these for me.

CORBACCIO. [*Finally reading the will.*] Mosca the heir!

VOLPONE. [*Aside.*]   O, his four eyes have found it.

CORBACCIO. I am cosened, cheated, by a parasite slave.
    Harlot, t'ast gulled me.

MOSCA.   Yes, sir. Stop your mouth,   65
    Or I shall draw the only tooth is left.
    Are not you he, that filthy, covetous wretch
    With the three legs, that here, in hope of prey,
    Have, any time this three year, snuffed about
    With your most grov'ling nose, and would have hired   70
    Me to the pois'ning of my patron, sir?
    Are not you he that have today in court
    Professed the disinheriting of your son?
    Perjured yourself? Go home, and die, and stink.
    If you but croak a syllable, all comes out.   75
    Away, and call your porters! Go, go stink.

    [*Exit* CORBACCIO.]

VOLPONE. [*Aside.*] Excellent varlet!

VOLTORE.   Now, my faithful Mosca,
    I find thy constancy.

MOSCA.   Sir?

VOLTORE.   Sincere.

MOSCA. [*Writing.*]   *A table*
    Of porphyry – I mar'l you'll be thus troublesome.   79

VOLTORE. Nay, leave off now, they are gone.

MOSCA.   Why, who are you?
    What! Who did send for you? O, cry you mercy,
    Reverend sir! Good faith, I am grieved for you,
    That any chance of mine should thus defeat

Your (I must needs say) most deserving travails;
But I protest, sir, it was cast upon me,   85
And I could almost wish to be without it,
But that the will o' th' dead must be observed.
Marry, my joy is that you need it not;
You have a gift, sir (thank your education)
Will never let you want while there are men   90
And malice to breed causes. Would I had
But half the like, for all my fortune, sir.
If I have any suits (as I do hope,
Things being so easy and direct, I shall not)
I will make bold with your obstreperous aid –   95
Conceive me, for your fee, sir. In meantime,
You that have so much law, I know ha' the conscience
Not to be covetous of what is mine.
Good sir, I thank you for my plate; 'twill help
To set up a young man. Good faith, you look   100
As you were costive; best go home and purge, sir.

[*Exit* VOLTORE.]

VOLPONE. [*Coming from behind the curtain.*] Bid him eat lettuce well!
    My witty mischief,
Let me embrace thee. O, that I could now
Transform thee to a Venus! Mosca, go,
Straight take my habit of *clarissimo*,   105
And walk the streets; be seen, torment 'em more.
We must pursue as well as plot. Who would
Have lost this feast?

MOSCA.   I doubt it will lose them.

VOLPONE. O, my recovery shall recover all.
    That I could now but think on some disguise   110
    To meet 'em in, and ask 'em questions.
    How I would vex 'em still at every turn!

MOSCA. Sir, I can fit you.

VOLPONE.   Canst thou?

MOSCA.   Yes, I know

One o' th' *commandatori*, sir, so like you;
  Him will I straight make drunk, and bring you his habit .   115

VOLPONE. A rare disguise, and answering thy brain!
  O, I will be a sharp disease unto 'em.

MOSCA. Sir, you must look for curses –

VOLPONE.   Till they burst;
  The fox fares ever best when he is cursed. [*Exeunt.*]

Act V, Scene iv

[*Enter*] PEREGRINE [*disguised, and*] three MERCHANTS.

[PEREGRINE.] Am I enough disguised?

1 MERCHANT.   I warrant you.

PEREGRINE. All my ambition is to fright him only.

2 MERCHANT. If you could ship him away, 'twere excellent.

3 MERCHANT. To Zant or to Aleppo?

PEREGRINE.   Yes, and have's
  Adventures put i' th' *Book of Voyages*,   5
  And his gulled story registered for truth?
  Well, gentlemen, when I am in a while,
  And that you think us warm in our discourse,
  Know your approaches.

1 MERCHANT.   Trust it to our care.

  [*Exeunt* MERCHANTS. *Enter* WOMAN.]

PEREGRINE. Save you, fair lady. Is Sir Pol within?   10

WOMAN. I do not know, sir.

PEREGRINE.   Pray you, say unto him
  Here is a merchant upon earnest business
  Desires to speak with him.

WOMAN.   I will see, sir.

PEREGRINE.   Pray you.

   [Exit WOMAN.]

I see the family is all female here.

   [Re-enter WOMAN.]

WOMAN. He says, sir, he has weighty affairs of state   15
   That now require him whole; some other time
   You may possess him.

PEREGRINE.   Pray you, say again,
   If those require him whole, these will exact him
   Whereof I bring him tidings.

   [Exit WOMAN.]

                       What might be
   His grave affair of state now? How to make   20
   Bolognian sausages here in Venice, sparing
   One o' th' ingredients?

   [Re-enter WOMAN.]

WOMAN.   Sir, he says he knows
   By your word 'tidings' that you are no statesman,
   And therefore wills you stay.

PEREGRINE.   Sweet, pray you return him:
   I have not read so many proclamations   25
   And studied them for words, as he has done,
   But – Here he deigns to come.

   [Enter SIR POL.]

SIR POLITIC.   Sir, I must crave
   Your courteous pardon. There hath chanced today
   Unkind disaster 'twixt my lady and me,
   And I was penning an apology   30
   To give her satisfaction, as you came now.

PEREGRINE. Sir, I am grieved I bring you worse disaster:
   The gentleman you met at th' port today,
   That told you he was newly arrived –

SIR POLITIC.   Ay, was
   A fugitive punk?

PEREGRINE.   No, sir, a spy, set on you,   35
   And he has made relation to the Senate
   That you professed to him to have a plot
   To sell the state of Venice to the Turk.

SIR POLITIC. O me!

PEREGRINE.   For which warrants are signed by this time
   To apprehend you and to search your study   40
   For papers –

SIR POLITIC.   Alas, sir, I have none but notes
   Drawn out of play-books –

PEREGRINE.   All the better, sir.

SIR POLITIC. And some essays. What shall I do?

PEREGRINE. Sir, best
   Convey yourself into a sugar-chest,
   Or, if you could lie round, a frail were rare;   45
   And I could send you aboard.

SIR POLITIC.   Sir, I but talked so
   For discourse sake, merely.

   They knock without.

PEREGRINE.   Hark, they are there.

SIR POLITIC. I am a wretch, a wretch!

PEREGRINE.   What will you do, sir?
   Ha' you ne'er a currant-butt to leap into?
   They'll put you to the rack; you must be sudden.   50

SIR POLITIC. Sir, I have an engine –

3 MERCHANT. [*Off-stage.*]   Sir Politic Would-be!

2 MERCHANT. [*Off-stage.*] Where is he?

SIR POLITIC.   That I have thought upon beforetime.

PEREGRINE. What is it?

SIR POLITIC.   – I shall ne'er endure the torture! –
    Marry, it is, sir, of a tortoise-shell,
    Fitted for these extremities. Pray you, sir, help me.   55
    [*Getting into the shell.*] Here I've a place, sir, to put back my legs;
    Please you to lay it on, sir. With this cap
    And my black gloves, I'll lie, sir, like a tortoise
    Till they are gone.

PEREGRINE.   And call you this an engine?   59

SIR POLITIC. Mine own device – Good sir, bid my wife's women
    To burn my papers.

    [*Exit* WOMAN. *The three* MERCHANTS] *rush in.*

1 MERCHANT.   Where's he hid?

3 MERCHANT.   We must,
    And will, sure, find him.

2 MERCHANT.   Which is his study?

1 MERCHANT.   What
    Are you, sir?

PEREGRINE.   I'm a merchant that came here
    To look upon this tortoise.

3 MERCHANT.   How!

1 MERCHANT.   St Mark!
    What beast is this?

PEREGRINE.   It is a fish.

2 MERCHANT. [*Striking the shell.*] Come out here!   65

PEREGRINE. Nay, you may strike him, sir, and tread upon him.
    He'll bear a cart.

1 MERCHANT.   What, to run over him?

PEREGRINE.   Yes.

3 MERCHANT. Let's jump upon him.

2 MERCHANT.   Can he not go?

PEREGRINE.   He creeps, sir.

1 MERCHANT. Let's see him creep.

PEREGRINE.   No, good sir, you will hurt him.

2 MERCHANT. Heart, I'll see him creep, or prick his guts.   70

3 MERCHANT. Come out here!

PEREGRINE. [*Aside to* SIR POL.] Pray you, sir. Creep a little.

1 MERCHANT.   Forth!

2 MERCHANT. Yet further.

PEREGRINE.   Good sir! [*Aside to* SIR POL.] Creep!

2 MERCHANT.   We'll see his legs.

   They pull off the shell and discover him.

3 MERCHANT. Godso, he has garters!

1 MERCHANT.   Ay, and gloves!

2 MERCHANT.   Is this
   Your fearful tortoise?

PEREGRINE. [*Throwing off his disguise.*] Now, Sir Pol, we are even.
   For your next project I shall be prepared.   75
   I am sorry for the funeral of your notes, sir.

1 MERCHANT. 'Twere a rare motion to be seen in Fleet Street!

2 MERCHANT. Ay, i' the term.

1 MERCHANT.   Or Smithfield, in the fair.

3 MERCHANT. Methinks 'tis but a melancholic sight!

PEREGRINE. Farewell, most politic tortoise.

   [*Exeunt* PEREGRINE *and* MERCHANTS. *Enter* WOMAN.]

SIR POLITIC.   Where's my lady?   80
   Knows she of this?

WOMAN.   I know not, sir.

SIR POLITIC.   Inquire

[*Exit* WOMAN.]

O, I shall be the fable of all feasts,
The freight of the *gazetti*, ship-boys' tale,
And, which is worst, even talk for ordinaries.

[*Re-enter* WOMAN.]

WOMAN. My lady's come most melancholic home,   85
    And says, sir, she will straight to sea, for physic.

SIR POLITIC. And I, to shun this place and clime forever,
    Creeping with house on back, and think it well
    To shrink my poor head in my politic shell. [*Exeunt.*]

Act V, Scene v

[*Enter*] VOLPONE [*and*] MOSCA: *the first in the habit of a commandatore,
the other, of a clarissimo.*

[VOLPONE.] Am I then like him?

MOSCA.   O sir, you are he;
    No man can sever you.

VOLPONE.   Good.

MOSCA.   But what am I?

VOLPONE. 'Fore heav'n, a brave *clarissimo*; thou becomest it!
    Pity thou wert not born one.

MOSCA.   If I hold
    My made one, 'twill be well.

VOLPONE.   I'll go and see   5
    What news first at court. [*Exit.*]

MOSCA.   Do so. My fox
    Is out on his hole, and ere he shall re-enter,
    I'll make him languish in his borrowed case,
    Except he come to composition with me.

Androgyno, Castrone, Nano!

[*Enter* ANDROGYNO,CASTRONE, *and* NANO.]

ALL.   Here.   10

MOSCA. Go, recreate yourselves abroad; go, sport.

   [*Exeunt* ANDROGYNO,CASTRONE, *and* NANO.]

   So, now I have the keys and am possessed.
   Since he will needs be dead afore his time,
   I'll bury him, or gain by him. I'm his heir,
   And so will keep me till he share, at least.   15
   To cozen him of all were but a cheat
   Well placed; no man would construe it a sin:
   Let his sport pay for't. This is called the Fox-trap. [*Exit.*]

Act V, Scene vi

[*Enter*] CORBACCIO [*and*] CORVINO.

[CORBACCIO.] They say the court is set.

CORVINO.   We must maintain
   Our first tale good, for both our reputations.

CORBACCIO. Why, mine's no tale; my son would there have killed
      me!

CORVINO. That's true, I had forgot. Mine is, I am sure.
   But for your will, sir. –

CORBACCIO.   Ay, I'll come upon him   5
   For that hereafter, now his patron's dead.

   [*Enter* VOLPONE *disguised.*]

VOLPONE. Signor Corvino! And Corbaccio! [*To* CORVINO.] Sir,
   Much joy unto you.

CORVINO.   Of what?

VOLPONE.   The sudden good

Dropped down upon you –

CORBACCIO.   Where?

VOLPONE.   – And none knows how.
   [*To* CORBACCIO.] From old Volpone, sir.

CORBACCIO.   Out, arrant knave!   10

VOLPONE. Let not your too much wealth, sir, make you furious.

CORBACCIO. Away, thou varlet.

VOLPONE.   Why, sir?

CORBACCIO.   Dost thou mock me?

VOLPONE. You mock the world, sir; did you not change wills?

CORBACCIO. Out, harlot!

VOLPONE.   O! Belike you are the man,
   Signor Corvino? Faith, you carry it well;   15
   You grow not mad withal. I love your spirit:
   You are not over-leavened with your fortune.
   You should ha' some would swell now like a wine-vat
   With such an autumn – Did he gi' you all, sir?

CORVINO. Avoid, you rascal.

VOLPONE.   Troth, your wife has shown   20
   Herself a very woman! But you are well;
   You need not care; you have a good estate
   To bear it out, sir: better by this chance.
   Except Corbaccio have a share?

CORBACCIO.   Hence, varlet.

VOLPONE. You will not be a'known, sir; why, 'tis wise: 25
   Thus do all gamesters, at all games, dissemble;
   No man will seem to win.

   [*Exeunt* CORVINO *and* CORBACCIO.]

                   Here comes my vulture,
   Heaving his beak up i' the air, and snuffing.

Act V, Scene vii

[*Enter to him*] VOLTORE.

[VOLTORE.] Outstripped thus by a parasite! a slave!
   Would run on errands! and make legs for crumbs!
   Well, what I'll do –

VOLPONE.   The court stays for your worship.
   I e'en rejoice, sir, at your worship's happiness,
   And that it fell into so learned hands,   5
   That understand the fingering –

VOLTORE.   What do you mean?

VOLPONE. I mean to be a suitor to your worship
   For the small tenement out of reparations,
   That at the end of your long row of houses
   By the Piscaria; it was in Volpone's time,   10
   Your predecessor, ere he grew diseased,
   A handsome, pretty, customed bawdy-house
   As any was in Venice – none dispraised –
   But fell with him. His body and that house
   Decayed together.

VOLTORE.   Come, sir, leave your prating.   15

VOLPONE. Why, if your worship give me but your hand
   That I may ha' the refusal, I have done.
   'Tis a mere toy to you, sir, candle-rents;
   As your learned worship knows –

VOLTORE.   What do I know?

VOLPONE. Marry, no end of your wealth, sir, God decrease it!   20

VOLTORE. Mistaking knave! What, mock'st thou my misfortune?

VOLPONE. His blessing on your heart, sir; would 'twere more!

   [*Exit* VOLTORE.]

   Now to my first again, at the next corner.

Act V, Scene viii

[*Enter to him*] CORVINO [*and*] CORBACCIO. MOSCA *passes* [*across the stage, before them*].

[CORBACCIO.] See, in our habit! See the impudent varlet!

CORVINO. That I could shoot mine eyes at him like gunstones!

    [*Exit* MOSCA.]

VOLPONE. But is this true, sir, of the parasite?

CORBACCIO. Again, t'afflict us? Monster!

VOLPONE.   In good faith, sir,
  I'm heartily grieved a beard of your grave length   5
  Should be so over-reached. I never brooked
  That parasite's hair; methought his nose should cozen.
  There still was somewhat in his look did promise
  The bane of a *clarissimo*.

CORBACCIO.   Knave –

VOLPONE.   Methinks
  Yet you, that are so traded i' the world,   10
  A witty merchant, the fine bird Corvino,
  That have such moral emblems on your name,
  Should not have sung your shame and dropped your cheese,
  To let the fox laugh at your emptiness.

CORVINO. Sirrah, you think the privilege of the place   15
  And your red, saucy cap, that seems to me
  Nailed to your jolt-head with those two *chequins*,
  Can warrant your abuses. Come you hither:
  You shall perceive, sir, I dare beat you. Approach.

VOLPONE. No haste, sir. I do know your valour well,   20
  Since you durst publish what you are, sir.

CORVINO.   Tarry,
  I'd speak with you.

VOLPONE.   Sir, sir, another time –

CORVINO. Nay, now.

VOLPONE.   O God, sir! I were a wise man
  Would stand the fury of a distracted cuckold.

  MOSCA [*enters and*] *walks by them* [*again*].

CORBACCIO. What, come again!

VOLPONE. [*Aside.*]   Upon 'em, Mosca; save me.   25

CORBACCIO. The air's infected where he breathes.

CORVINO.   Let's fly him.

  [*Exeunt* CORVINO *and* CORBACCIO.]

VOLPONE. Excellent basilisk! Turn upon the vulture.

Act V, Scene ix

[*Enter to them*] VOLTORE.

[VOLTORE.] Well, flesh-fly, it is summer with you now;
  Your winter will come on.

MOSCA.   Good advocate,
  Pray thee not rail, nor threaten out of place thus;
  Thou'lt make a solecism, as Madam says.
  Get you a biggen more; your brain breaks loose. [*Exit.*]   5

VOLTORE. Well, sir

VOLPONE.   Would you ha' me beat the insolent slave?
  Throw dirt upon his first good clothes?

VOLTORE.   This same
  Is doubtless some familiar!

VOLPONE.   Sir, the court,
  In troth, stays for you. I am mad a mule
  That never read Justinian should get up   10
  And ride an advocate. Had you no quirk
  To avoid gullage, sir, by such a creature?
  I hope you do but jest; he has not done't:
  This's but confederacy to blind the rest.

You are the heir?

VOLTORE.   A strange, officious,   15
  Troublesome knave! Thou dost torment me.

VOLPONE.   I know –
  It cannot be, sir, that you should be cozened;
  'Tis not within the wit of man to do it.
  You are so wise, so prudent – [*Following, as* VOLTORE *leaves.*]
      and 'tis fit
  That wealth and wisdom still should go together –   20

  [*Exeunt.*]

Act V, Scene x

[*Enter*] *four* AVOCATORI, NOTARIO, COMMANDATORI,
BONARIO, CELIA, CORBACCIO, CORVINO.

[1 AVOCATORE.] Are all the parties here?

NOTARIO.   All but the advocate.

2 AVOCATORE. And here he comes.

  [*Enter* VOLTORE, VOLPONE *following him.*]

[1] AVOCATORE.   Then bring 'em forth to sentence.

VOLTORE. O, my most honoured fathers, let your mercy
  Once win upon your justice, to forgive –
  I am distracted –

VOLPONE. [*Aside.*] What will he do now?

VOLTORE.   O,   5
  I know not which t'address myself to first,
  Whether your fatherhoods, or these innocents –

CORVINO. [*Aside.*] Will he betray himself?

VOLTORE.   Whom equally
  I have abused, out of most covetous ends –

CORVINO. The man is mad!

CORBACCIO.   What's that?

CORVINO.   He is possessed.   10

VOLTORE. For which, now struck in conscience, here I prostrate
    Myself at your offended feet for pardon. [*He kneels.*]

1, 2 AVOCATORI. Arise.

CELIA.   O heav'n, how just thou art!

VOLPONE. [*Aside.*]   I'm caught
    I' mine own noose –

CORVINO. [*Aside to* CORBACCIO.] Be constant, sir; nought now
    Can help but impudence.

1 AVOCATORE. [*To* VOLTORE.] Speak forward.

COMMANDATORE. [*To the courtroom.*]   Silence!   15

VOLTORE. It is not passion in me, reverend fathers,
    But only conscience, conscience, my good sires,
    That makes me now tell truth. That parasite,
    That knave, hath been the instrument of all –

[2] AVOCATORE. Where is that knave? Fetch him.   19

VOLPONE.   I go. [*Exit.*]

CORVINO.   Grave fathers,
    This man's distracted, he confessed it now,
    For, hoping to be old Volpone's heir,
    Who now is dead –

3 AVOCATORE.   How?

2 AVOCATORE.   Is Volpone dead?

CORVINO. Dead since, grave fathers –

BONARIO.   O, sure vengeance!

1 AVOCATORE.   Stay, –
    Then he was no deceiver?

VOLTORE.   O, no, none;   25
  The parasite, grave fathers –

CORVINO.   He does speak
  Out of mere envy, 'cause the servant's made
  The thing he gaped for. Please your fatherhoods,
  This is the truth; though I'll not justify
  The other but he may be some-deal faulty.   30

VOLTORE. Ay, to your hopes as well as mine, Corvino;
  But I'll use modesty. Pleaseth your wisdoms
  To view these certain notes, and but confer them;
  As I hope favour, they shall speak clear truth.

CORVINO. The devil has entered him!

BONARIO.   Or bides in you.   35

4 AVOCATORE. We have done ill, by a public officer
  To send for him, if he be heir.

2 AVOCATORE.   For whom?

4 AVOCATORE. Him that they call the parasite.

3 AVOCATORE.   'Tis true;
  He is a man of great estate now left.

4 AVOCATORE. [*To* NOTARIO.] Go you and learn his name,
    and say the court   40
  Entreats his presence here, but to the clearing
  Of some few doubts.

    [*Exit* NOTARIO.]

2 AVOCATORE.   This same's a labyrinth!

1 AVOCATORE. [*To* CORVINO.] Stand you unto your first
    report?

CORVINO. My state,
  My life, my fame –

BONARIO.   Where is't?

CORVINO.   Are at the stake.   44

1 AVOCATORE. [*To* CORBACCIO.] Is yours so too?

CORBACCIO.   The advocate's a knave,
  And has a forked tongue –

2 AVOCATORE.   Speak to the point.

CORBACCIO. So is the parasite too.

1 AVOCATORE.   This is confusion.

VOLTORE. [*Indicating the papers.*] I do beseech your fatherhoods,
  read but those.

CORVINO. And credit nothing the false spirit hath writ.
  It cannot be but he is possessed, grave fathers.   50

  [*They examine the papers.*]

Act V, Scene xi

[*Enter elsewhere on stage*] VOLPONE.

[VOLPONE.] To make a snare for mine own neck! And run
  My head into it wilfully! with laughter!
  When I had newly 'scaped, was free and clear!
  Out of mere wantonness! O, the dull devil
  Was in this brain of mine when I devised it,   5
  And Mosca gave it second; he must now
  Help to sear up this vein, or we bleed dead.

  [*Enter* NANO, ANDROGYNO, *and* CASTRONE.]

  How now! Who let you loose? Whither go you now?
  What? to buy gingerbread? or to drown kitlings?

NANO. Sir, Master Mosca called us out of doors,   10
  And bid us all go play, and took the keys.

ANDROGYNO.   Yes.

VOLPONE. Did Master Mosca take the keys? Why, so!
  I am farther in. These are my fine conceits!
  I must be merry, with a mischief to me!

What a vile wretch was I that could not bear   15
My fortune soberly! I must ha' my crotchets!
And my conundrums! Well, go you and seek him.
His meaning may be truer than my fear.
Bid him, he straight come to me to the court;
Thither will I, and if 't be possible,   20
Unscrew my advocate, upon new hopes:
When I provoked him, then I lost myself. [*Exeunt.*]

Act V, Scene xii

[*Four*] AVOCATORI, [NOTARIO, COMMANDATORI,
BONARIO, CELIA, VOLTORE, CORBACCIO, CORVINO].

[1 AVOCATORE.] [*With* VOLTORE*'s notes.*] These things can
     ne'er be reconciled. He here
   Professeth that the gentleman was wronged,
   And that the gentlewoman was brought thither,
   Forced by her husband, and there left.

VOLTORE.   Most true.

CELIA. How ready is heav'n to those that pray!

1 AVOCATORE.   But that   5
   Volpone would have ravished her he holds
   Utterly false, knowing his impotence.

CORVINO. Grave fathers, he is possessed; again, I say,
   Possessed. Nay, if there be possession and
   Obsession, he has both.

3 AVOCATORE.   Here comes our officer.   10

   [*Enter* VOLPONE *disguised.*]

VOLPONE. The parasite will straight be here, grave fathers.

4 AVOCATORE. You might invent some other name, sir varlet.

3 AVOCATORE. Did not the notary meet him?

VOLPONE.   Not that I know.

4 AVOCATORE. His coming will clear all.

2 AVOCATORE.   Yet it is misty.

VOLTORE. May 't please your fatherhoods –

    VOLPONE *whispers* [*to*] *the* ADVOCATE.

VOLPONE. [*Aside to* VOLTORE.]   Sir, the parasite   15
    Willed me to tell you that his master lives;
    That you are still the man; your hopes the same;
    And this was only a jest –

VOLTORE.   How?

VOLPONE.   Sir, to try
    If you were firm, and how you stood affected.

VOLTORE. Art sure he lives?

VOLPONE.   Do I live, sir?

VOLTORE.   O, me!   20
    I was too violent.

VOLPONE.   Sir, you may redeem it.
    They said you were possessed: fall down, and seem so.
    I'll help to make it good.

    VOLTORE *falls.*

                 God bless the man!
    [*Aside to* VOLTORE.] Stop your wind hard, and swell. [*Aloud.*]
      See, see, see, see!
    He vomits crooked pins! His eyes are set   25
    Like a dead hare's hung in a poulter's shop!
    His mouth's running away! [*To* CORVINO.] Do you see, Signor?
    Now 'tis in his belly –

CORVINO.   Ay, the devil!

VOLPONE. Now, in his throat –

CORVINO.   Ay, I perceive it plain.

VOLPONE. 'Twill out, 'twill out! Stand clear. See where it flies   30
    In shape of a blue toad with a bat's wings!
    [*To* CORBACCIO.] Do not you see it, sir?

CORBACCIO.   What? I think I do.

CORVINO. 'Tis too manifest.

VOLPONE.   Look! he comes t' himself!

VOLTORE. Where am I?

VOLPONE.   Take good heart, the worst is past, sir.
    You are dispossessed.

1 AVOCATORE.   What accident is this?   35

2 AVOCATORE. Sudden, and full of wonder!

3 AVOCATORE.   If he were
    Possessed, as it appears, all this is nothing.

    [*He indicate's* VOLTORE'*s statement.*]

CORVINO. He has been often subject to these fits.

1 AVOCATORE. Show him that writing. [*To* VOLTORE.] Do you
    know it, sir?

VOLPONE. [*Aside to* VOLTORE.] Deny it, sir, forswear it, know
    it not.   40

VOLTORE. Yes, I do know it well, it is my hand;
    But all that it contains is false.

BONARIO.   O practice!

2 AVOCATORE. What maze is this?

1 AVOCATORE.   Is he not guilty then,
    Whom you there name the parasite?

VOLTORE.   Grave fathers,
    No more than his good patron, old Volpone.   45

4 AVOCATORE. Why, he is dead!

VOLTORE.   O no, my honoured fathers,

He lives –

1 AVOCATORE. How! Lives?

VOLTORE.   Lives.

2 AVOCATORE.   This is subtler yet!

3 AVOCATORE. You said he was dead?

VOLTORE.   Never.

3 AVOCATORE. [*To* CORVINO.]   You said so?   49

CORVINO. I heard so.

4 AVOCATORE. Here comes the gentleman, make him way.

   [*Enter* MOSCA.]

3 AVOCATORE.   A stool!

4 AVOCATORE. A proper man! [*Aside.*] And, were Volpone dead,
   A fit match for my daughter.

3 AVOCATORE.   Give him way.

VOLPONE. [*Aside to* MOSCA.] Mosca, I was almost lost; the advocate
   Had betrayed all; but now it is recovered.
   All's o' the hinge again. Say I am living.

MOSCA. What busy knave is this? Most reverend fathers,   55
   I sooner had attended your grave pleasures,
   But that my order for the funeral
   Of my dear patron did require me –

VOLPONE. [*Aside.*]   Mosca!

MOSCA. Whom I intend to bury like a gentleman.

VOLPONE. [*Aside.*] Ay, quick, and cozen me of all.

2 AVOCATORE.   Still stranger!
   More intricate!

1 AVOCATORE. And come about again!   61

4 AVOCATORE. [*Aside.*] It is a match, my daughter is bestowed.

MOSCA. [*Aside to* VOLPONE.] Will you gi' me half?

VOLPONE. [*Half aloud.*]   First I'll be hang'd.

MOSCA. [*Aside.*]   I know
    Your voice is good, cry not so loud.

1 AVOCATORE.   Demand   65
    The advocate. Sir, did not you affirm
    Volpone was alive?

VOLPONE.   Yes, and he is;
    [*Indicating* MOSCA.] This gent'man told me so.
    [*Aside to* MOSCA.]   Thou shalt have half.

MOSCA. Whose drunkard is this same? Speak some that know him;
    I never saw his face. [*Aside to* VOLPONE.] I cannot now
    Afford it you so cheap.

VOLPONE. [*Aside.*]   No?

1 AVOCATORE. [*To* VOLTORE.] What say you?   70

VOLTORE. The officer told me.

VOLPONE.   I did, grave fathers,
    And will maintain he lives with mine own life,
    And that this creature told me. [*Aside.*] I was born
    With all good stars my enemies!

MOSCA.   Most grave fathers,
    If such an insolence as this must pass   75
    Upon me, I am silent; 'twas not this
    For which you sent, I hope.

2 AVOCATORE.   Take him away.

VOLPONE. [*Aside.*] Mosca!

3 AVOCATORE.   Let him be whipped.

VOLPONE. [*Aside.*]   Wilt thou betray me?
    Cozen me?

3 AVOCATORE. And taught to bear himself
    Towards a person of his rank.

4 AVOCATORE.   Away! [VOLPONE *is seized.*]   80

MOSCA. I humbly thank your fatherhoods.

VOLPONE. [*Aside.*]   Soft, soft. Whipped?
    And lose all that I have? If I confess,
    It cannot be much more.

4 AVOCATORE. [*To* MOSCA.] Sir, are you married?

VOLPONE. [*Aside.*] They'll be allied anon: I must be resolute.
    The fox shall here uncase.

He puts off his disguise.

MOSCA.   Patron!   85

VOLPONE.   Nay, now
    My ruins shall not come alone. Your match
    I'll hinder sure; my substance shall not glue you,
    Nor screw you, into a family.

MOSCA.   Why, patron!

VOLPONE. I am Volpone, and this [*indicating* MOSCA] is my knave;
    This [*indicating* VOLTORE], his own knave; this [*indicating*
        CORBACCIO], avarice's fool;   90
    This [*indicating* CORVINO], a chimera of wittol, fool, and knave.
    And, reverend fathers, since we all can hope
    Nought but a sentence, let's not now despair it.
    You hear me brief.

CORVINO.   May it please your fatherhoods –

COMMANDATORE.   Silence!

1 AVOCATORE. The knot is now undone by miracle!   95

2 AVOCATORE. Nothing can be more clear.

3 AVOCATORE.   Or can more prove
    These innocent.

1 AVOCATORE.   Give 'em their liberty.

BONARIO. Heaven could not long let such gross crimes be hid.

2 AVOCATORE. If this be held the highway to get riches,
    May I be poor!

3 AVOCATORE. This 's not the gain, but torment.   100

1 AVOCATORE. These possess wealth as sick men possess fevers,
    Which trulier may be said to possess them.

2 AVOCATORE. Disrobe that parasite.

CORVINO, MOSCA.   Most honoured fathers –

1 AVOCATORE. Can you plead aught to stay the course of justice?
    If you can, speak.

CORVINO, VOLTORE. We beg favour.

CELIA.   And mercy.   105

2 AVOCATORE. You hurt your innocence, suing for the guilty.
    Stand forth; and first the parasite. You appear
    T'have been the chiefest minister, if not plotter,
    In all these lewd impostures; and now, lastly,
    Have with your impudence abused the court,   110
    And habit of a gentleman of Venice,
    Being a fellow of no birth or blood:
    For which our sentence is, first thou be whipped;
    Then live perpetual prisoner in our galleys.

VOLPONE. I thank you for him.

MOSCA.   Bane to thy wolfish nature!   115

1 AVOCATORE. Deliver him to the *Saffi*. [MOSCA *is led off*.]
        Thou, Volpone,
    By blood and rank a gentleman, canst not fall
    Under like censure; but our judgment on thee
    Is that thy substance all be straight confiscate
    To the hospital of the Incurabili;   120
    And since the most was gotten by imposture,
    By feigning lame, gout, palsy, and such diseases,
    Thou art to lie in prison, cramped with irons,
    Till thou beest sick and lame indeed. Remove him.

VOLPONE. This is called mortifying of a fox.   125

   [*He is led aside.*]

1 AVOCATORE. Thou, Voltore, to take away the scandal
   Thou hast giv'n all worthy men of thy profession,
   Art banished from their fellowship, and our state.
   Corbaccio – bring him near – we here possess
   Thy son of all thy state, and confine thee   130
   To the monastery of San' Spirito;
   Where, since thou knew'st not how to live well here,
   Thou shalt be learned to die well.

CORBACCIO.   Ha! What said he?

COMMANDATORE. You shall know anon, sir.

[1] AVOCATORE.   Thou, Corvino, shalt
   Be straight embarked from thine own house, and rowed   135
   Round about Venice, through the Grand Canale,
   Wearing a cap with fair long ass's ears
   Instead of horns; and so to mount, a paper
   Pinned on thy breast, to the Berlino –

CORVINO.   Yes,
   And have mine eyes beat out with stinking fish,   140
   Bruised fruit, and rotten eggs – 'Tis well: I'm glad
   I shall not see my shame yet.

1 AVOCATORE.   And to expiate
   Thy wrongs done to thy wife, thou art to send her
   Home to her father with her dowry trebled.
   And these are all your judgments –

ALL.   Honoured fathers!   145

1 AVOCATORE. Which may not be revoked. Now you begin,
   When crimes are done and past and to be punished,
   To think what your crimes are. Away with them.
   Let all that see these vices thus rewarded
   Take heart, and love to study 'em! Mischiefs feed   150
   Like beasts till they be fat, and then they bleed. [*Exeunt.*]

[The Epilogue]

[VOLPONE.] The seasoning of a play is the applause.
   Now, though the fox be punished by the laws,
   He yet doth hope there is no suff'ring due
   For any fact which he hath done 'gainst you.
   If there be, censure him; here he doubtful stands;   5
   If not, fare jovially, and clap your hands.

The End.

This Comedy was first acted in the year 1605
by the King's Majesty's Servants.

The principal comedians were
Richard Burbage   John Hemminges
Henry Condell   John Lowin
William Sly   Alexander Cooke.
With the allowance of the Master of Revels.

140

Glossary

Alembics – equipment for distilling

Aurum palpabile – 'touchable gold', a punning reference to *aurum potabile* ('drinkable gold'), a medicine containing gold

Bagatine – a coin of low value

Balloo – a kind of ball game

Basilisk – mythical serpent able to kill with a glance

Battens – thrives

Bedlam – a corruption of 'Bethlehem', a London asylum for the insane

Berlina – stocks, pillory

Biggen – lawyer's wig or cap

Callet – prostitute

Canaglia – the lower orders of society

Cataplasm – medicinal poultice

Chequin – a Venetian gold coin

Chimera – a mythical beast, part lion, part serpent and part goat

Ciarlatani – quack doctors

Cittern – a stringed instrument

Clarissimo – Italian nobleman

Coadjutor – collaborator or helper

Commendatori – officers

Cope-man – trader

Culverin – a cannon or early musket

Defalk – cut or lop off: colloquially, to skim off a profit

Fleer – smile sycophantically

Frail – wicker or rush basket

Fricatrice – prostitute

Fucus – cosmetic reputedly made from seaweed

Gazet – Venetian coin of low denomination

Glebe – clergyman's land; poetically, a place of fertile growth

Gorecrow – carrion crow

Gull – one who can be fooled, is 'gullible'

Hernia ventosa – 'windy guts', flatulence

Hoy – a small coastal trading boat

Iliaca passio – stomach-ache

Mal-caduco – fits, epilepsy

Mallows – one of several varieties of leafy vegetable

Moccenigo – coin of the lowest value

Moyle – mule

Mummia – medicine supposedly made from Egyptian mummies

Oppilations – blockages

Osteraa – inn

Pescheria – fish market

Phthisic – disease of the lungs, such as asthma or tuberculosis

Pistolet – a gold coin

Primero – a card game

Punk – prostitute

Ordinary – eating place

Pythagoras – Greek philosopher who maintained that after death the
    soul migrated to another body

Quacksalvers – quack doctors

Quean – prostitute

Rochet – a species of fish

Romagnaa – a Greek wine, noted for its sweetness

Saffi – officers of the court

Salt – lascivious

Scartoccios – wrapping papers, eg for medicines

Scotomy – loss of sight

Shambles – abbatoirs

Simples – ingredients for medicine

Sols – gold coins

Stale – decoy

Strangury – disease of the bladder

Strappado – form of punishment in which the victim was dropped from
    a height, his or her fall checked only by ropes tied to the wrists

Tires – clothes

Tremor cordia – heart palpitations

Trigon – triangle

Unguenteo – medicinal ointment

Visor – mask

Wittol – cuckold

Sly for code

212-947-8844

SF2DML6

865